The Complete Ninja Speedi

Recipe Book for Beginners

Easy Ninja Speedi Cookbook for Beginners to Create Gourmet Meals with Varied Cooking Modes

Isabella Sykes

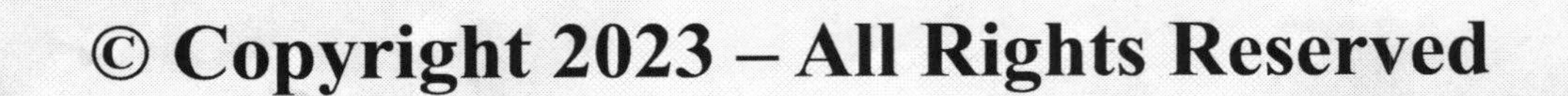

Contents

Introduction

There are few undeclared rules when it comes to cooking meals. It needs to be quick, it needs to be mouthwatering, and it needs to be healthy for you. You are thinking, "It is impossible." No, it is super easy to simultaneously prepare quick, delicious, and healthy food. It is possible due to Ninja Speedi Rapid Cooker and Air Fryer. Yes, this cooking appliance is the perfect choice if you want healthy and quick food at dinner.

This cooking appliance will take you less time and prepare yummy food. When you have no time for cooking, this cooking appliance will become your best companion. In my cookbook, I included different recipes for you; you can cook them in this appliance easily. But, you think, "How will I use Ninja Speedi Rapid Cooker and Air Fryer"? Many tricky questions will come to your mind. Don't so worry; I am here to solve your questions. In my cookbook, you will get guidance about "how to use Ninja Speedi Rapid Cooker and Air Fryer"? How many buttons it have, and many more? I will give you the answer to every question in detail. In my cookbook, I added simple and delicious recipes for you. You will get step-by-step cooking instructions and a final dish picture also. Slice and dice the vegetables and add them to the cooking pot, adjust the cooking time, temperature, and go to your work. Boom! You will get delicious food on your table in very less time.

The Ninja speedi rapid cooker and air fryer has multiple cooking modes. You can choose your favorite mode or according to food requirement and start cooking different meals for your family.
The benefit of this cooking appliance is that you can prepare food very fast within fifteen minutes only. This is amazing equipment.

Fundamentals of Ninja Speedi Rapid Cooker & Air Fryer

What is Ninja Speedi Rapid Cooker & Air Fryer?

Ninja Speedi Rapid Cooker and Air Fryer are advanced cooking equipment. It provides many cooking functions. If you are using rapid cooker functions, then you have speedi meals, steam, and crisp, steam and bake, steam, and proof cooking functions; if you are using air fry/ stovetop functions, then you have an air fryer, roast/ bake, broil, dehydrate, sear/sauté, slow cooker, and sous vide cooking function. You can use these essential cooking functions according to your need. For example, if you want to prepare crispy chicken nuggets, you can use an air fryer cooking function. If you want to prepare it in less, then you can use steam and crisp cooking. It is super easy to use. Choosing the right cooking mode helps to cook the perfect food.
There are two types of processes in this appliance:

1. Rapid cook:

This process is best for cooking whole roasts, root veggies, fresh and frozen proteins, and two-part dinners.

Steam and Crisp	Proof
Steam and Bake	Steam
Speedi Meals	

2. Air fryer/Stovetop

Sous Vide	Sear/Sauté
Slow Cook	Broil
Air Fry	Dehydrate
Roast/Bake	

You can use this cooking appliance everyday and cooking mouthwatering and healthy food for your family and friends. Share meals with your friends and enjoy compliments.

Benefits of Using Ninja Speedi Rapid Cooker & Air Fryer

There are a lot of benefits of using Ninja Speedi Rapid Cooker and Air Fryer cooking appliances. Some are given below:

Easy-to-make different meals:

Using Ninja Speedi Rapid Cooker and Air Fryer, you can prepare different meals, such as chicken roast, beef, leg of lamb, fresh and frozen veggies, fruits, desserts, snacks, appetizers, and many more. Every type of meal you want to cook on your special days. This cooking appliance is super convenient.

Super simple cleaning process:

Some people didn't know how to clean the Ninja appliance and got confused, but now you didn't need to worry about it. I added a step-by-step cleaning process for the Ninja speedi rapid cooker and air fryer. So go ahead and see below. It is super easy. Note: don't use harsh chemicals to clean it. It can damage your equipment.

Multiple modes:

Ninja speedi rapid cooker and air fryer have so many cooking functions. You can select your favorite cooking

mode onto the equipment and prepare your favorite food. These are the followings: Speedi meals, steam and crisp, steam and bake, steam, proof, air fry, roast/bake, broil, dehydrate, sear/sauté, slow cook, and sous vide.

Easy and quick food:

Using a rapid cooker, you can prepare quick food. You can use this cooking process if you have no time to cook food. Using this cooking process, you can use speedi meals, steam, and crisp, steam and bake, steam, and proof cooking functions.

How to Use Ninja Speedi Rapid Cooker & Air Fryer?

It is super easy to use Ninja Speedi Rapid Cooker and Air Fryer. You need to read instructions deeply and completely. You will immediately learn how to use this cooking appliance.

Parts and Accessories of Ninja Speedi Rapid Cooker & Air Fryer

These are essential parts and accessories of this appliance. For cooking food, you need to use these accessories. These are the followings:

Crisper tray: Upper and bottom position

Removable cooking pot: It is about 6-quart and easily removable.

Cooker lid: It is simple to close and open while holding the handle, which is present in the middle front of the unit.

Control panel: It will guide you on the cooking time and temperature of the food.

Cooker base: You will add food to the cooker base to cook meals.

Lid handle: It is present in the centre-front of the cooking appliance.

Unit lid: When using an air fryer/stovetop or rapid cooker cooking mode, you can easily handle or open the unit lid while cooking food to check the tenderness.

Heating element: It is present under the lid, and it will help to cook your food.

Air outlet vent: It removes the steam while cooking food.

Condensation collector: Drainage moisture is collected in this condensation collector.

Accessory and Assembly Instructions Using Smart Lid

Crispy tray:

There are two positions of the crispy tray: The upper position and the bottom position. The upper position is used for veggies and proteins when following the recipe instructions for Air Broil or if you are using Speedi meals. The bottom position is used for steam and air fryer.

How to use it: If you want to set up the Crisper tray in the upper position, first rotate the leg of the crisper tray outwards so that it extends past the four corners of the crisper tray. The legs should sit at the base of each groove, and the tray will remain elevated in the pot.

Note: Before putting the Crisper tray in the upper position, add the ingredients needed at the bottom of the pot. If there is the instruction for Speedi meals in the recipes, then you should set up the crisper tray in the elevated position.

If you want to set up the Crisper tray in the bottom position, you should rotate the legs of the crisper tray so that it is turned against the underside of the tray. The tray will remain at the bottom of the pot.

It's time to use the smart switch: The smart switch allows you to change the cook modes: Air fry/stovetop and Rapid cooker. The smart switch will determine which cooking function you want to select for cooking food.

How to open and close the lid: The handle is present in the middle front of the appliance, just above the control panel. You can easily hold the handle to open and close the lid of the unit. You can close and open the lid using the Smart switch, whether using air fryer/ stovetop or rapid cooker cooking mode.

Main Functions of Ninja Speedi Rapid Cooker & Air Fryer

There are twelve cooking functions in the appliance. You can select any one of these cooking mode and prepare your favorite food.

Rapid Cooker

Speedi Meals: If your family is big, you can use this option. With one touch, you can prepare two-part meals for your family. It cooks food quickly, within 15 minutes. This option is perfect for those who have no time to cook food. Examples: Green bean casserole, Salmon cake, Chicken thighs, Creamy garlic pasta, Quinoa rice, Leg of lamb, Beef wellington, and many more.

Steam and crisp: If you want to eat quick, juicy, and crispy food, you can use this cooking mode. This cooking mode gives the food crispiness and juicy taste. Example: Crispy kale fritter, salmon cake, Chicken nuggets, crispy cheese rolls, and many more.

Steam & bake: If you want to eat baked, crispy, and quick food, you should use this cooking function. Example: Banana bread, muffins, brownies, baked chicken pasta, baked chicken breast, cookies, and many more. The benefit of this cooking mode is that you can bake food with less fat.

Steam: Using this cooking mode, you can cook delicate food at high temperatures. Examples: Salmon, lamb, eggs, mushrooms, spinach, and seaweed. Steam eliminates the extra oils from the food and keeps it moist.

Proof: This cooking mode provides low heat to maintain the environment to raise the yeast/dough. For example, grow the dough for bread, brownies, cookies and many more.

Air Fry/Stovetop Cooking Process

Air fry: An air fryer is the best option if you want to eat crispy and crunchy food with very little oil. You can prepare a lot of food using the air fryer cooking mode. Example: Meatballs, Chicken nuggets, Chicken wings, roasted cauliflower, stuffed mushrooms, onion rings, fried shrimp, fish sticks, kebabs, steaks, and many more.

Bake/roast: This cooking mode is just like an oven. You can roast proteins like beef, chicken, lamb, and meat and baked treats like doughnuts, cookies, and bread. Use the bake/roast cooking function to make everything from the main dish to appetizer and sides.

Broil: You can use it to caramelize and brown the tops of the food as if you have prepared baked bread or any other food, and you to get brown tops over it, you can select broil cooking mode and start broiling the food. Use broil cooking mode to make meat crispier, cheesier and live better. With broil, you are cooking food directly under high heat.

Dehydrate: Dehydrate is a perfect cooking mode to dehydrate fruits, veggies, meats, and healthy snacks. You can make yummy jerks, dried fruits, and vegetable chips. It takes a lot of time to dehydrate the food for about hours, but it gives delicious food. You can preserve many foods after dehydrating. These are the best foods to dehydrate: Fruits like blueberries, cherries, apples, pears, bananas, apricot, peaches etc. Vegetables like tomatoes, peas, onions, beans, carrots, mushrooms etc.

Sauté/sear: This cooking mode is just like you are cooking food on the stovetop in the skillet or pan. You can prepare soup, sauces, sautéing veggies, and browning meats, using sear and sauté cooking mode. Every cooking needs searing and sautéing at some stage; Ninja speedi rapid cooker and air fryer offer sear/sauté mode to ease cooking.

Slow cook: This cooking function is the perfect choice if you are a busy woman and have no time to stand for a whole day in the kitchen. You can use it for cooking food at a very low temperature for a long time. You can adjust the cooking time and temperature and go to your work. After a few hours, you will get delicious, healthy and tender food. You can prepare stews, soups, and meats using this cooking mode. It takes a lot of time to cook food, but it also tastes great.

Sous vide: The word sous vide means under vacuum. It is a process of vacuum-sealing food into the bag and cooking it at a precise temperature in the water bath. It is a process of sealing food into an air-tight container. It yields delicious flavor and is perfect for making tender meats and veggies.

Buttons and User Guide of Ninja Speedi Rapid Cooker & Air Fryer

SmartSwitch: SmartSwitch is used to move up and down to switch between air fry/stovetop and rapid cooker cooking mode. The operating button is available for all cooking modes.

Center arrows: When you have chosen a cooking mode using a smartswitch, use the center arrows to scroll through the options until your desired function is highlighted.

Left arrow: This arrow is used to adjust the cooking temperature. Use the up and down arrows to adjust the cooking temperature of your food. In the recipe, the cooking temperature is mentioned.

Right arrow: The right arrow is used to adjust the cooking time. Use the up and down arrows to adjust the cooking time for your food. In the recipe, cooking time is mentioned.

Start/stop button: Press start/stop button to start cooking. When you press the button again while the unit is cooking the food, it will stop the current cooking function. You can open the lid and check the tenderness of the food. After this, close the lid and press the start button again to start cooking.

Power: When cooking is done, press the power button to shuts the unit off and stops all cooking functions.

Using the Ninja Speedi Rapid Cooker & Air Fryer

Using the Rapid Cooker Functions

To turn on the cooking appliance, plug the power cord into the wall outlet and press the power button near the temperature button.

Speedi Meals:

- First of all, remove the Crisper Tray from the bottom of the cooking pot before getting started.
- Then, according to the recipe instructions, add the required ingredients and liquid to the bottom of the pot.
- After that, pull out the legs on the Crisper tray and put the Crisper tray in the upper position into the cooking pot. Add required ingredients onto the tray according to the recipe instructions.
- Turn the SmartSwitch to Rapid cooker and press the center arrows to choose Speedi meals. It will show on display. Use up and down arrows at the left of the display to choose/adjust the cooking temperature from 250 degrees Fahrenheit to 450 degrees Fahrenheit, in either 10 or 15 degrees increments. You can choose the temperature according to the recipe instructions.
- Then, use the arrows at the right of the display to choose/adjust the cooking time in one minute increments up to 30 minutes. You can select cooking time according to the recipe instructions.
- After that, press the start/stop button to start the cooking process.
- The unit has a display screen that shows you the progress bars and indicates the unit is building steam.
- When the cooking appliance reaches the precise steam level, the cooking timer will start counting down.
- When cooking time is completed, the unit will beep, and the display shows "End" on the screen. If food needs more time to cook, use the arrows to the right of the display and add more time to it. The cooking

appliance will leave out preheating.

- Note: When cooking time is completed, remove the vegetables or protein from the Crisper tray. Also, remove the Crisper tray with silicone-tipped tongs.

Steam and Crisp:

- Prepare the ingredients according to the recipe instructions.
- Turn the SmartSwitch to Rapid cooker and press the center arrows to choose Steam and crisp. It will show on display. Use up and down arrows at the left of the display to choose/adjust the cooking temperature from 250 degrees Fahrenheit to 450 degrees Fahrenheit, in either 10 or 15 degrees increments. You can choose the temperature according to the recipe instructions.
- Then, use the arrows at the right of the display to choose/adjust the cooking time in one minute increments up to 30 minutes. You can select cooking time according to the recipe instructions.
- After that, press the start/stop button to start the cooking process.
- The unit has a display screen that shows you the progress bars and indicates the unit is building steam.
- When the cooking appliance reaches the precise steam level, the cooking timer will start counting down.
- When cooking time is completed, the unit will beep, and the display shows "End" on the screen. If food needs more time to cook, use the arrows to the right of the display and add more time to it. The cooking appliance will leave out preheating.
- Note: When cooking time is completed, remove the food from the Crisper tray. Also, remove the Crisper tray with silicone-tipped tongs.

Steam and bake:

- Ensure the Crisper tray is at the bottom of the cooking pot. Place the baking accessories on the top of the Crisper tray.
- Turn the SmartSwitch to Rapid cooker and press the center arrows to choose Steam and bake. It will show on display. Use up and down arrows at the left of the display to choose/adjust the cooking temperature from 250 degrees Fahrenheit to 400 degrees Fahrenheit, in either 10 or 15 degrees increments. You can choose the temperature

according to the recipe instructions.

- Then, use the arrows at the right of the display to choose/adjust the cooking time in one minute increments up to 30 minutes. You can select cooking time according to the recipe instructions.
- After that, press the start/stop button to start the cooking process.
- The unit has a display screen that shows you the progress bars and indicates the unit is building Steam.
- When the cooking appliance reaches the precise steam level, the cooking timer will start counting down.
- The unit will beep when cooking time is completed, and the display shows "End" on the screen. If food needs more time to cook, use the arrows to the right of the display and add more time to it. The cooking appliance will leave out preheating.
- Note: When cooking time is completed, remove the food from the Crisper tray. Also, remove the Crisper tray with silicone-tipped tongs.

Steam:

- To start the process, add the water to the bottom of the cooking pot. Ensure the Crisper tray is at the bottom of the cooking pot. Then, add the required ingredients to it according to the recipe instructions.
- Turn the SmartSwitch to Rapid cooker and press the center arrows to choose Steam. It will show on display.
- Then, use the arrows at the right of the display to choose/adjust the cooking time in one minute increments up to 30 minutes. You can select cooking time according to the recipe instructions.
- After that, press the start/stop button to start the

cooking process.

- Note: This cooking function has no temperature adjustment.
- The unit has a display screen that shows you the progress bars and indicates the unit is building Steam.
- The unit will start preheating and allow it to boil the liquid. The unit has a display screen that shows you the progress bars and indicates the unit is building Steam. When preheating is completed, the cooking timer will start counting down. It will show until it reaches the desired temperature, and then the display will show the timer counting down.
- The unit will beep when cooking time is completed, and the display shows "End" on the screen. If food needs more time to cook, use the arrows to the right of the display and add more time to it. The cooking appliance will leave out preheating.
- Note: When cooking time is completed, remove the vegetables or protein from the Crisper tray. Also, remove the Crisper tray with silicone-tipped tongs.

Proof:

- Ensure the Crisper tray is at the bottom of the cooking pot.
- Place the dough to the baking accessory and put it on the top of the Crisper tray.
- Turn the SmartSwitch to Rapid cooker and press the center arrows to choose Steam and bake. It will show on display. Use up and down arrows at the left of the display to choose/adjust the cooking temperature from 90 degrees Fahrenheit to 105 degrees Fahrenheit, in 5 degrees increments. You can choose the temperature according to the recipe instructions.
- Then, use the arrows at the right of the display to choose/adjust the cooking time of proof from 15 minutes to 4 hours, in five minutes increments. You can select cooking time according to the recipe instructions.
- After that, press the start/stop button to start the cooking process.
- The unit has a display screen that shows you the progress bars.
- The unit will beep when cooking time is completed, and the display shows "End" on the screen.

Using the Air Fry/Stovetop Functions:

Air Fry:

- Ensure the Crisper tray is at the bottom of the cooking pot.
- According to the recipe instructions, add required ingredients to the pot and close the lid.
- Turn the SmartSwitch to Rapid cooker and press the center arrows to choose air fry. It will show on display. Use up and down arrows at the left of the display to choose/adjust the cooking temperature from 250 degrees Fahrenheit to 400 degrees Fahrenheit, in either 10 or 15 degrees increments. You can choose the temperature according to the recipe instructions.
- Then, use the arrows at the right of the display to choose/adjust the cooking time in minute increments up to 1 hour. You can select cooking time according to the recipe instructions.
- After that, press the start/stop button to start the cooking process.
- Note: If you want to get best results, it is recommended that shake the ingredients during the air frying process. Open the lid and remove the pot from the unit. Shake it well and put it back to the unit and close the lid. The cooking will start automatically when you will close the lid.
- The unit will beep when cooking time is completed, and the display shows "End" on the screen.

Bake/Roast:

- Ensure the Crisper tray is at the bottom of the cooking pot.
- Turn the SmartSwitch to Rapid cooker and press the center arrows to choose bake/roast. It will show on

display. Use up and down arrows at the left of the display to choose/adjust the cooking temperature from 300 degrees Fahrenheit to 400 degrees Fahrenheit, in either 10 or 15 degrees increments. You can choose the temperature according to the recipe instructions.

- Then, use the arrows at the right of the display to choose/adjust the cooking time up to 1 hour in 1 minute increment and from 1 hour to 4 hours in 5 minutes increments. You can select cooking time according to the recipe instructions.
- After that, press the start/stop button to start the cooking process.
- The unit has a display screen that shows you the progress bars.
- The unit will beep when cooking time is completed, and the display shows "End" on the screen.

Broil:

- Ensure the Crisper tray is at the upper position of the cooking pot.
- According to the recipe instructions, add required ingredients to the pot and close the lid.
- Turn the SmartSwitch to Rapid cooker and press the center arrows to choose broil. It will show on display. Use up and down arrows at the left of the display to choose/adjust the cooking temperature from 400 degrees Fahrenheit to 450 degrees Fahrenheit, in either 25 degrees increments. You can choose the temperature according to the recipe instructions.
- Then, use the arrows at the right of the display to choose/adjust the cooking time up to 30 minutes in 1 minute increment. You can select cooking time according to the recipe instructions.
- After that, press the start/stop button to start the cooking process.
- The unit has a display screen that shows you the progress bars.
- The unit will beep when cooking time is completed, and the display shows "End" on the screen.

Dehydrate:

- Ensure the Crisper tray is at the bottom of the cooking pot.
- Turn the SmartSwitch to Rapid cooker and press the center arrows to choose "dehydrate". It will show on display. Use up and down arrows at the left of the display to choose/adjust the cooking temperature from 105 degrees Fahrenheit to 195 degrees Fahrenheit. You can choose the temperature according to the recipe instructions.
- Then, use the arrows at the right of the display to choose/adjust the cooking time between 1 and 12 hours, in 15 minutes increments. You can select cooking time according to the recipe instructions.
- After that, press the start/stop button to start the cooking process.
- The unit has a display screen that shows you the progress bars.
- The unit will beep when cooking time is completed, and the display shows "End" on the screen.

Sear/sauté:

- First of all, remove the Crisper Tray from the bottom of the cooking pot before getting started.
- According to the recipe instructions, add the required ingredients to the pot and close the lid.
- Turn the SmartSwitch to Rapid cooker and press the center arrows to choose sear/sauté. It will show on display. Use up and down arrows at the left of the display to choose/adjust "Lo1," "2," "3," "4," or "Hi5."
- Note: Using the sear/sauté cooking function, there is no cooking time adjustment.
- Press the start/stop button to start the cooking. The timer will start counting up.
- Press the start/stop button to stop the sear/sauté cooking mode. If you want to use the different cooking functions, press the start/stop button to stop the cooking function and use the smartswitch and middle-front arrows to choose desired cooking function.
- Note: You can use this function whether the lid is

open or close.

- Note: Use only non-stick utensils in the whole meal process. Don't use metal utensils because they will scratch the non-stick coating on the cooking pot.
- Remember: The cooking function "Sear/Sauté" will automatically turn off after one hour for "4" and "Hi5" and four hours for "LO1," "2," and "3."

Sous vide:

- To get the best results, don't use the unit prior, and also don't use hot water.
- First, remove the Crisper Tray from the bottom of the cooking pot before getting started.
- Add 12 cups of room temperature water to the cooking pot. Close the lid.
- Turn the SmartSwitch to Rapid cooker and press the center arrows to choose "sous vide." It will show on display. Use up and down arrows at the left of the display to choose/adjust the cooking temperature in 5 degrees increments from 120 degrees Fahrenheit to 190 degrees Fahrenheit. You can choose the temperature according to the recipe instructions.
- The cooking will default to three hours. Use the arrows at the right of the display to choose/adjust the cooking time in 15-minute increments up to 12 hours, then 1-hour increments from 12 hours to 24 hours. You can select cooking time according to the recipe instructions.
- Press the start/stop button to start preheating.
- Note: The preheating time depends on the temperature of the water added. Meanwhile, gather three pounds of ingredients and season them with the required ingredients. Put each portion into the single-use re-sealable plastic bags. Use a double-bag for each portion of food or wrap it into the plastic wrap before putting them into the single-use re-sealable plastic bag because it will cook for four plus hours with a temperature above 160 degrees Fahrenheit. It will protect the food during a long time of submersion.
- The cooking equipment will beep when preheating is completed. The display will show "ADD FOOD" on the screen. Then, open the lid and add the bags to the water using the water displacement process: If you are working with one bag at a time, leave a corner of the bag unzipped. Lower the bag slowly into the water, and the pressure of the water will

push the air out of the bag. When the seal of the bag is above the water line, stop closing the bag. Make sure that there is no water on gets inner side. Then, close the lid.

- The unit will beep when cooking time is completed, and the display shows "End" on the screen.
- Note: If you want to reheat the food that has been cooked using sous vide cooking mode, use the sous vide cooking function again.
- When water is preheating, add food into the re-sealable bags and cook for 15 to 20 minutes at the desired temperature. Sous vide is the first cooking step, and food should be finished by using a dry heat method such as air frying, roasting, broiling, or sautéing.

Slow cook:

- First of all, remove the Crisper Tray from the bottom of the cooking pot before getting started.
- According to the recipe instructions, add the required ingredients to the pot and close the lid.
- Turn the SmartSwitch to Rapid cooker and press the center arrows to choose "slow cook." It will show on display. Use up and down arrows at the left of the display to choose/adjust the "Hi," "Lo," or "bUFFEt." You can choose the temperature according to the recipe instructions.
- The cooking will default to three hours. Use the arrows at the right of the display to choose/adjust the cooking time.
- Note: The slow cook BUFFET time setting may be adjusted between two to twelve hours. The slow cook, LO time setting may be adjusted between six to twelve hours. The slow HI time setting may be adjusted between four to twelve hours.

- Press the start/stop button to start cooking.
- When the cooking time reaches zero, the cooking appliance will beep and automatically turn to KEEP WARM mode and start counting up.

Cleaning and Maintenance Process of Ninja Speedi Rapid Cooker & Air Fryer

It is important that the unit should be cleaned completely after every use. It will protect your equipment and run for a long time.

- First, unplug the unit from the wall outlet and ensure that the unit is cooled before washing.
- When the unit is cooled, clean the control panel and cooker base with a clean damp cloth. Please don't put the unit into the dishwasher or don't immerse it in any liquid.
- If any food residue is stuck into the cooking pot, crisper tray, and bake accessory, fill it with water and allow it to soak before cleaning.
- Don't use harsh or scouring pads to remove the stuck food. Always use a non-abrasive cleanser or liquid dish soap with a nylon pad or brush.
- When all parts get dry, return them to the unit.

Cleaning process:

- Turn smartswitch to Rapid cooker.
- Choose "Steam" cooking mode and adjust the cooking time to 10 minutes. Close the lid. Press the start/stop button.
- When the time reaches zero, and the unit has cooled down, use a sponge or wet cloth to wipe down the interior of the lid.
- Alert: When cleaning the lid, don't touch the fan.
- Then, remove the water from the pot and rinse the crisper tray and cooking pot to remove the residues.

NOTE:

- You should use the above cleaning instructions if you see any residue or stuck oil onto the heating element or fan. Wipe down the interior of the lid to avoid causing burning.

Instructions for Your Protection

- Don't put the unit near the gas or heating element like a stovetop or heated oven.
- Before using the unit, make sure that the appliance is assembled properly.
- Don't immerse the main unit into the liquid or dishwasher.
- Don't allow your children to play with the unit.
- When the empty meal pot, don't heat it for more than ten minutes.
- Don't use this appliance for deep-frying.
- Allow the unit to cool before cleaning.
- Don't use rapid cooker functions without adding water or ingredients to the bottom of the pot.
- This unit is not used for making instant rice.

Troubleshooting

- There is a lot of steam coming from the appliance when using the steam function.
- Answer: It is normal to release steam come out from the unit when using the steam function.
- "ERR" message appears onto the display.
- Answer: The unit is not working properly. Contact Customer Service.
- The unit is counting up rather than down.
- Answer: The cooking time is completed, now the unit is in KEEP WARM mode.

4-Week Diet Plan

Week 1

Day 1:

Breakfast: Banana Oatmeal
Lunch: Garlic White Zucchini Rolls
Snack: Honey Carrot Pieces
Dinner: Crusted Chicken
Dessert: Roasted Pecan Clusters

Day 2:

Breakfast: Mushroom-Spinach Frittata
Lunch: Parmesan Artichokes
Snack: Onion Potato Totes
Dinner: Black Cod Fillets
Dessert: Brownies

Day 3:

Breakfast: Savory Bread Pudding
Lunch: Cheese Zucchini & Cauliflower Fritters
Snack: Zucchini Sticks
Dinner: Honey Mustard Ham
Dessert: Cinnamon Pretzels

Day 4:

Breakfast: Baked Eggs with Bacon
Lunch: Simple Spaghetti Squash
Snack: Cumin Carrots
Dinner: Garlicky Chicken Wings
Dessert: Keto Danish

Day 5:

Breakfast: Egg-Loaded Potato
Lunch: Easy Spaghetti Squash Alfredo
Snack: Easy Cheese Sticks
Dinner: Salmon Eggs Mix
Dessert: Coconut Cake

Day 6:

Breakfast: Coffee Donuts
Lunch: Spinach Cheese Pie
Snack: Breaded Onion Rings
Dinner: Baked Sausage
Dessert: Chocolate Banana Bread

Day 7:

Breakfast: Vegetable Taco Wraps
Lunch: Broccoli Pizza
Snack: Veggie Dish
Dinner: Onion Stuffed Turkey Balls
Dessert: Carrot Cake

Week 2

Day 1:

Breakfast: Bistro Potato Wedges
Lunch: Italian Egg and Veggies
Snack: Tofu Cubes
Dinner: Tuna Cube Wraps
Dessert: Lime Cheesecake

Day 2:

Breakfast: Breaded Spinach Balls
Lunch: BBQ Mushrooms
Snack: Eggplant Fries
Dinner: Stuffed Beef Meatballs
Dessert: Chocolate Brownies

Day 3:

Breakfast: Chicken Sandwich
Lunch: Carrot Fries
Snack: Honey Sweet Potato Bites
Dinner: Avocado Turkey Burrito
Dessert: Raspberry Pies

Day 4:

Breakfast: Bacon & Horseradish
Lunch: Garlic Green Beans & Mushrooms
Snack: Simple Kale Chips
Dinner: Cilantro-Lime Shrimp
Dessert: Blueberry Clafoutis

Day 5:

Breakfast: Cheese Vegetable Toast
Lunch: Corn Fritters
Snack: Vegetable Stuffed Tomatoes
Dinner: Spiced Baby Back Ribs
Dessert: Stuffed Nectarines

Day 6:

Breakfast: Vanilla Cinnamon Toasts
Lunch: Brussels Sprouts with Almonds
Snack: Spiced Mix Nuts
Dinner: Turkey Patties
Dessert: Banana Boats

Day 7:

Breakfast: Peanut Butter Bread Slices
Lunch: Balsamic-Soy Mushrooms
Snack: Cheese Potatoes
Dinner: Savory Tilapia Fillets
Dessert: Sour Cream Cake

Week 3

Day 1:
Breakfast: Savory Avocado Eggs
Lunch: Quartered Artichoke Hearts
Snack: Baked Potatoes with Parsley
Dinner: Bacon Sliders
Dessert: Easy Peach Cobbler

Day 2:
Breakfast: Avocado Tempura in Juice
Lunch: Beet Chips
Snack: Seasoned Baby Corn
Dinner: Savory Tilapia Fillets
Dessert: Strawberry Shortcake

Day 3:
Breakfast: Potato Nuggets
Lunch: Spiced Baby Potatoes
Snack: Roasted Fresh Ears of Corn
Dinner: Garlic Rack of Lamb
Dessert: Cheese Shortbread Cookies

Day 4:
Breakfast: Spiced Bread Rolls
Lunch: Potato Pancakes
Snack: Roasted Carrot Chunks
Dinner: Vegetable & Chicken Kebabs
Dessert: Pumpkin Cake

Day 5:
Breakfast: Vegetable Frittata
Lunch: Spicy Zucchini Boats
Snack: Fried Kale Pieces
Dinner: Savory Tilapia Fillets
Dessert: Lime Butter Bars

Day 6:
Breakfast: Maple Buns
Lunch: Coated Eggplant Slices
Snack: Curry Cauliflower
Dinner: Parmesan Pork Chops
Dessert: Chocolate Cake

Day 7:
Breakfast: Taj Tofu with Sesame Seeds
Lunch: Baked Russet Potatoes
Snack: Green Beans in Lemon Juice
Dinner: Hamburger Steak
Dessert: Fried Biscuit Donuts

Week 4

Day 1:
Breakfast: Tasty Paper Bacon
Lunch: Cauliflower Bites in Buffalo Sauce
Snack: Broccoli Florets with Sesame Seeds
Dinner: Philly Chicken Cheesesteak
Dessert: Vanilla Chocolate Soufflé

Day 2:
Breakfast: Delicious Posh Soufflé
Lunch: Green Tomatoes
Snack: Panko Avocado Fries
Dinner: Fish Vegetable Tacos
Dessert: Fried Bananas

Day 3:
Breakfast: Muffin Sandwich
Lunch: Roasted Parmesan Zucchini
Snack: Spinach Samosa
Dinner: Tuscan Pork Kebabs
Dessert: Apple Hand Pies

Day 4:
Breakfast: Chicken Pea Delight
Lunch: Fried Cabbage
Snack: Large Tomato Halves
Dinner: Bacon-Wrapped Chicken
Dessert: Blueberry Muffins

Day 5:
Breakfast: French Bread Toast
Lunch: Stuffed Peppers
Snack: Vegetable Fritters with Cheese
Dinner: Coconut Shrimp
Dessert: Cream Wontons

Day 6:
Breakfast: Bacon Quiche with Cheese
Lunch: Tofu Broccoli Bowls
Snack: Honey Carrot Pieces
Dinner: Tangy Beef Meatballs
Dessert: Cherry Bars

Day 7:
Breakfast: Chorizo Risotto
Lunch: Stuffed Tomatoes
Snack: Zucchini Sticks
Dinner: Tandoori Chicken with Yogurt
Dessert: Cinnamon Bananas

Chapter 1 Breakfast Recipes

Eggs with Spinach

Prep Time: 8 minutes | Cook Time: 20 minutes | Serves: 4

1 tablespoon avocado oil
½ teaspoon chili flakes
6 eggs, beaten
2 cups spinach, chopped

1. Brush the mold with avocado oil. Mix chili flakes with eggs and spinach in a bowl, and then pour the mixture in the mold. 2. Place the Crisper Tray in the bottom position. Add the mold to the tray and close the lid. 3. Move SmartSwitch to AIR FRY/STOVETOP, and then use the center front arrows to select BAKE/ROAST. 4. Set the cooking temperature to 365 degrees F and the cooking time to 20 minutes. 5. Serve warm.
Per Serving: Calories 130; Fat 9.89g; Sodium 116mg; Carbs 1.19g; Fiber 0.5g; Sugar 0.33g; Protein 8.77g

Cream Cauliflower Frittata

Prep Time: 10 minutes | Cook Time: 15 minutes | Serves: 4

4 eggs, beaten
1 tablespoon cream cheese
½ cup heavy cream
½ cup cauliflower, chopped
½ teaspoon chili flakes
½ teaspoon avocado oil

1. In the mixing bowl, mix eggs with cream cheese, heavy cream, and chili flakes. 2. Brush the Crisper Tray with avocado oil and put the cauliflower inside. Flatten it in one layer. 3. Place the Crisper Tray in the bottom position. Close the lid. Move SmartSwitch to AIR FRY/STOVETOP, and then use the center front arrows to select BAKE/ROAST. Set the cooking temperature to 370 degrees F and the cooking time to 14 minutes. 4. Serve and enjoy.
Per Serving: Calories 152; Fat 12.61g; Sodium 116mg; Carbs 1.79g; Fiber 0.4g; Sugar 1.04g; Protein 7.91g

Egg Turkey Mix

Prep Time: 10 minutes | Cook Time: 25 minutes | Serves: 2

1 pound ground turkey
2 teaspoons avocado oil
2 cups of coconut milk
1 cup Monterey jack cheese, shredded
2 eggs, beaten
1 teaspoon ground black pepper

1. Brush the pot with avocado oil. Mix ground turkey with coconut milk, cheese, eggs, and ground black pepper in the cooking pot with crisper tray, and flatten the mixture gently. 2. Move SmartSwitch to AIR FRY/STOVETOP. Set the cooking temperature to 370 degrees F and the cooking time to 25 minutes. 3. Serve and enjoy.
Per Serving: Calories 836; Fat 54.06g; Sodium 695mg; Carbs 13.16g; Fiber 0.3g; Sugar 12.82g; Protein 74.08g

Pleasy Breakfast Sandwich

Prep Time: 15 minutes | Cook Time: 15 minutes | Serves: 2

1 (8-ounce) package firm or extra-firm tofu, thinly sliced into rectangles or squares
2 teaspoons nutritional yeast, divided
¼ teaspoon sea salt, divided
⅛ teaspoon freshly ground black pepper, divided
Cooking oil spray (sunflower, safflower, or refined coconut)
4 slices bread
Cheesy Sauce
Vegan tempeh bacon (optional)
Vegan mayo, your choice (optional)
Leaf lettuce, dill pickles, and thinly sliced red onion (optional)

1. Place the tofu slices in a single layer on a plate and sprinkle evenly with 1 teaspoon nutritional yeast, ⅛ teaspoon salt, and half of the black pepper. Turn them over and sprinkle the remaining yeast, salt, and pepper on top. 2. Spray the Crisper Tray with the oil and place the tofu pieces in a single layer on it. Spray the tops with the oil. Bake them at 390 degrees F for 14 minutes. 3. Flip the tofu pieces halfway through cooking. Toast the bread, and top with the tofu slices, Cheesy Sauce, vegan meat (if using), and any additional toppings. 4. Devour immediately.
Per Serving: Calories 228; Fat: 8.15g; Sodium: 801mg; Carbs: 24.63g; Fiber: 2.3g; Sugar: 3.65g; Protein: 16.5g

Cream Egg Cups

Prep Time: 10 minutes | Cook Time: 5 minutes | Serves: 2

2 eggs
1 tablespoon cream cheese
1 teaspoon smoked paprika

1. Crack the eggs into the ramekins and top them with smoked paprika and cream cheese, and then arrange them on the Crisper Tray. 2. Place the Crisper Tray in the bottom position. Add the food to the pot and close the lid. Move SmartSwitch to AIR FRY/STOVETOP, and then use the center front arrows to select BAKE/ROAST. Set the cooking temperature to 400 degrees F and the cooking time to 3 minutes. 3. Serve and enjoy.
Per Serving: Calories 373; Fat 25.4g; Sodium 379mg; Carbs 2.63g; Fiber 0.4g; Sugar 1.28g; Protein 31.22g

Eggs over Bell Peppers

Prep Time: 5 minutes | Cook Time: 20 minutes | Serves: 4

2 bell peppers, sliced
4 eggs, beaten
1 teaspoon avocado oil
½ teaspoon white pepper

1. Brush the inside of cooking pot with avocado oil. Mix the bell peppers with white pepper in the pot with the tray. Pour the beaten eggs over the bell peppers. 2. Close the lid. Move SmartSwitch to AIR FRY/STOVETOP. Set the cooking temperature to 360 degrees F and the cooking time to 20 minutes. 3. Serve and enjoy.
Per Serving: Calories 83; Fat 5.36g; Sodium 64mg; Carbs 2.65g; Fiber 0.4g; Sugar 1.31g; Protein 6.01g

Egg Bacon Cups

Prep Time: 10 minutes | Cook Time: 10 minutes | Serves: 3

3 eggs
½ teaspoon ground paprika
3 bacon slices
1 teaspoon avocado oil
1 teaspoon chives, chopped

1. Brush the ramekins with avocado oil. Arrange the bacon slices in every ramekin in the shape of the circle, and then place them on the Crisper Tray. 2. Place the Crisper Tray in the bottom position. Add the ramekins to the pot and close the lid. Move SmartSwitch to AIR FRY/STOVETOP, and then use the center front arrows to select BAKE/ROAST. Set the cooking temperature to 370 degrees F and the cooking time to 10 minutes. 3. Crack the eggs in the center of every ramekin and adjust the cooking time to 365 degrees F after 7 minutes of cooking time. 4. Sprinkle the cooked eggs with chives and ground paprika.
Per Serving: Calories 183; Fat 15.95g; Sodium 185mg; Carbs 0.76g; Fiber 0.1g; Sugar 0.43g; Protein 8.85g

Toasts Cups

Prep Time: 12 minutes | Cook Time: 10 minutes | Serves: 2

⅓ cup coconut flour
1 egg, beaten
¼ teaspoon baking powder
2 teaspoons Erythritol
¼ teaspoon ground cinnamon
1 teaspoon mascarpone
1 tablespoon butter, softened

1. In the mixing bowl, mix coconut flour with egg, baking powder, Erythritol, ground cinnamon, and mascarpone. Grease the baking cups with butter and pour the coconut flour mixture inside. 2. Transfer the cups to the Crisper Tray. Place the Crisper Tray in the bottom position and close the lid. Move SmartSwitch to AIR FRY/STOVETOP, and then use the center front arrows to select BAKE/ROAST. Set the cooking temperature to 365 degrees F and the cooking time to 9 minutes. 3. Serve and enjoy.
Per Serving: Calories 123; Fat 10.66g; Sodium 139mg; Carbs 2.57g; Fiber 0.6g; Sugar 1.37g; Protein 4.84g

Potato Flautas with Fresh Salsa

Prep Time: 20 minutes | Cook Time: 8 minutes | Serves: 2

1 medium potato, peeled and chopped into small cubes (1½ cups chopped potato)
2 tablespoons nondairy milk, plain and unsweetened
2 large garlic cloves, minced or pressed
¼ teaspoon sea salt
⅛ teaspoon freshly ground black pepper
2 tablespoons minced scallions
4 sprouted corn tortillas
Cooking oil spray (sunflower, safflower, or refined coconut)
Fresh salsa
Guacamole or fresh avocado slices (optional)
Cilantro, minced (optional)

1. Cook the potato cubes in a pot over high heat for 15 minutes or until they are tender. Transfer the cooked potato cubes to a bowl and mash with a fork or potato masher. 2. Add the milk, garlic, salt, and pepper and stir well. Add the scallions and stir them into the mixture. Set the bowl aside. 3. Run the tortillas under water for a second, and then place them on the Crisper Tray and air-fry them at 390 degrees F for 1 minute. 4. Transfer the tortillas to a flat surface, laying them out individually. Place an equal amount of the potato filling in the center of each tortilla. 5. Roll the tortilla sides up over the filling and arrange them seam-side down on the Crisper Tray. 6. Spray the tops with oil, and then air-fry them at 390 degrees F for 7 minutes or until the tortillas are golden-browned and lightly crisp. 7. Serve the dish with sauce or salsa, and any of the additional options as desired.

Per Serving: Calories 427; Fat: 16.92g; Sodium: 402mg; Carbs: 65.11g; Fiber: 14.2g; Sugar: 3.81g; Protein: 9.4g

Cod Fish Sticks

Prep Time: 15 minutes | Cook Time: 10 minutes | Serves: 4

8 oz. cod fillet
1 egg, beaten
2 tablespoons coconut shred
1 teaspoon dried oregano
½ teaspoon salt
1 teaspoon avocado oil

1. Cut the cod fillet into sticks. Mix salt with dried oregano and coconut shred. 2. Dip the cod sticks in the beaten egg and coat in the coconut shred mixture. 3. Sprinkle the cod sticks with avocado oil. Place the Crisper Tray in the bottom position. 4. Add the ingredients to it and close the lid. Move SmartSwitch to AIR FRY/STOVETOP, set the cooking temperature to 400 degrees F and the cooking time to 10 minutes.

Per Serving: Calories 67; Fat 2.43g; Sodium 486mg; Carbs 0.53g; Fiber 0.2g; Sugar 0.25g; Protein 10.12g

Pimiento Cheese Tots

Prep Time: 15 minutes | Cook Time: 90 minutes | Serves: 4

2 medium russet potatoes, scrubbed
1 tablespoon olive oil
2 tablespoons butter, room temperature
4 tablespoons finely diced peeled yellow onion
½ cup pimento cheese
2 tablespoons gluten-free all-purpose flour
1 teaspoon salt
½ teaspoon ground black pepper

1. Prick each potato four times with tines of a fork. Rub olive oil evenly over potatoes. Place them on the Crisper Tray. AIR-FRY the potatoes at 400 degrees F for 45 minutes. 2. When done, let them rest in a plate for about 10 minutes until cool enough to handle. Scoop cooled potato flesh into a medium bowl. 3. Discard skins. Add butter, onion, pimento cheese, flour, salt, and pepper. Smash together ingredients until smooth. Tightly form a tablespoon-sized amount of potato mixture into a tot shape. 4. Repeat twenty-four times with remaining mixture. Add one-third of tots to Crisper Tray lightly greased with preferred cooking oil. 5. Brush tots with oil. Air-fry them at 400 degrees F for 15 minutes. Transfer the food to a plate and repeat two more times with remaining tots. 6. Let the cooked tots sit for 3 minutes until cool enough to handle. Use fingers to press cooled tots back into shape. 7. Serve warm.

Per Serving: Calories 311; Fat: 14.8g; Sodium: 797mg; Carbs: 37.75g; Fiber: 2.8g; Sugar: 1.69g; Protein: 8.43g

Cheddar Eggs

Prep Time: 5 minutes | Cook Time: 25 minutes | Serves: 4

4 eggs, beaten
1 teaspoon avocado oil
2 oz. Cheddar cheese, shredded

1. Brush the ramekins with avocado oil. Mix eggs with cheese and pour the mixture inside ramekins. 2. Place the Crisper Tray in the bottom position. Place the ramekins on the tray and close the lid. Move SmartSwitch to AIR FRY/STOVETOP, and then use the center front arrows to select BAKE/ROAST. Set the cooking temperature to 355 degrees F and the cooking time to 25 minutes. 3. Serve and enjoy.

Per Serving: Calories 98; Fat 6.57g; Sodium 219mg; Carbs 6g; Fiber 1.83g; Sugar 1.16g; Protein 7.43g

Easy Noochy Tofu

Prep Time: 10 minutes | Cook Time: 15 minutes | Serves: 4

1 (8-ounce) package firm or extra-firm tofu
4 teaspoons tamari or shoyu
1 teaspoon onion granules
½ teaspoon garlic granules
½ teaspoon turmeric powder
¼ teaspoon freshly ground black pepper
2 tablespoons nutritional yeast
1 teaspoon dried rosemary
1 teaspoon dried dill
2 teaspoons arrowroot (or cornstarch)
2 teaspoons neutral-flavored oil (such as sunflower, safflower, or melted refined coconut)
Cooking oil spray (sunflower, safflower, or refined coconut)

1. Cut the tofu into slices and press out the excess water. Cut the tofu into ½-inch cubes and place them in a bowl. Sprinkle the cubes with the tamari and toss gently to coat. Set aside for a few minutes. 2. Toss the tofu again, then add the onion, garlic, turmeric, and pepper. Gently toss them to thoroughly coat the cubes. Add the nutritional yeast, rosemary, dill, and arrowroot. 3. Toss gently to coat. Drizzle with the oil and toss one last time. Spray the Crisper Tray with the oil. Place the Crisper Tray in the bottom position. 4. Place the cubes on the tray and close the lid. Move SmartSwitch to AIR FRY/STOVETOP, and then use the center front arrows to select BAKE/ROAST. 5. Set the cooking temperature to 390 degrees F and the cooking time to 14 minutes. Lightly flip the tofu cubes halfway through baking. 6. When cooked, the outsides of the tofu cubes should be crisp and browned.

Per Serving: Calories 108; Fat: 3.65g; Sodium: 569mg; Carbs: 11.74g; Fiber: 1.9g; Sugar: 4.86g; Protein: 9.03g

Blueberry Cobbler

Prep Time: 5 minutes | Cook Time: 15 minutes | Serves: 4

⅓ cup whole-wheat pastry flour
¾ teaspoon baking powder
Dash sea salt
⅓ cup unsweetened nondairy milk
2 tablespoons maple syrup
½ teaspoon vanilla
Cooking oil spray (sunflower, safflower, or refined coconut)
½ cup blueberries
¼ cup granola, plain, or Gorgeous Granola
Nondairy yogurt (for topping, optional)

1. In a medium bowl, whisk together the flour, baking powder, and salt. Add the milk, maple syrup, and vanilla and whisk gently, just until thoroughly combined. 2. Spray a suitable baking pan with cooking oil and pour the mixture into the pan, using a rubber spatula so you don't leave any goodness behind. 3. Top evenly with the blueberries and granola. Place the Crisper Tray in the bottom position. Place the pan on the tray and close the lid. 4. Move SmartSwitch to AIR FRY/STOVETOP, and then use the center front arrows to select BAKE/ROAST. Set the cooking temperature to 350 degrees F and the cooking time to 15 minutes. 5. Enjoy plain or topped with a little nondairy vanilla yogurt.

Per Serving: Calories 168; Fat: 3.63g; Sodium: 93mg; Carbs: 31.51g; Fiber: 2.3g; Sugar: 17.77g; Protein: 3.62g

Cheese Bacon Balls

Prep Time: 10 minutes | Cook Time: 12 minutes | Serves: 4

10 oz. bacon, chopped
1 teaspoon dried dill
4 teaspoons cream cheese
1 teaspoon dried oregano

1. Place the Crisper Tray in the bottom position. Add the bacon to it and close the lid. 2. Move SmartSwitch to AIR FRY/STOVETOP, set the cooking temperature to 375 degrees F and the cooking time to 12 minutes. 3. Flip the bacon from time to time to avoid burning. When cooked, mix bacon with remaining ingredients and make the balls. Enjoy.
Per Serving: Calories 237; Fat 22.44g; Sodium 1060mg; Carbs 5.12g; Fiber 2.1g; Sugar 0.19g; Protein 8.03g

Granola Apple Oatmeal

Prep Time: 5 minutes | Cook Time: 20 minutes | Serves: 2

De-light-full caramelized apples
¾ cup rolled oats
1½ cups water
Nondairy vanilla-flavored milk of your choice, unsweetened
½ cup granola, or Gorgeous Granola

1. Make the de-light-full caramelized apples recipe. 2. Once the apples have been cooking for about 10 minutes, begin making the oatmeal: In a medium pot, bring the oats and water to a boil, and then reduce to low heat. Simmer them, stirring often, until all of the water is absorbed. 3. Place the oatmeal into two bowls. Pour a small amount of nondairy milk on top. Place the Crisper Tray in the bottom position. 4. Place the bowls on the tray and close the lid. Move SmartSwitch to AIR FRY/STOVETOP, and then use the center front arrows to select BAKE/ROAST. Set the cooking temperature to 390 degrees F and the cooking time to 10 minutes. 5. Once done, add the cooked apples on top of the oatmeal, and top with granola. Eat while warm.
Per Serving: Calories 357; Fat: 11.68g; Sodium: 169mg; Carbs: 67.27g; Fiber: 10.1g; Sugar: 25.87g; Protein: 10.88g

Cheese Chicken Muffins

Prep Time: 10 minutes | Cook Time: 10 minutes | Serves: 6

1 cup ground chicken
½ cup Cheddar cheese, shredded
1 teaspoon dried oregano
½ teaspoon salt
1 tablespoon butter, softened
1 teaspoon dried parsley
2 tablespoons coconut flour

1. Mix all ingredients in the mixing bowl and stir until homogenous. Pour the muffin mixture in the muffin molds. 2. Place the Crisper Tray in the bottom position. Place the molds on the tray and close the lid. Move SmartSwitch to AIR FRY/STOVETOP, and then use the center front arrows to select BAKE/ROAST. Set the cooking temperature to 375 degrees F and the cooking time to 10 minutes. 3. Serve and enjoy.
Per Serving: Calories 393; Fat 28.75g; Sodium 393mg; Carbs 0.46g; Fiber 0.1g; Sugar 0.17g; Protein 31.24g

Multi-Spiced Eggs

Prep Time: 10 minutes | Cook Time: 20 minutes | Serves: 4

8 eggs
1 teaspoon dried basil
1 teaspoon ground black pepper
1 teaspoon dried oregano
1 teaspoon avocado oil

1. Brush the Crisper Tray with avocado oil from inside. 2. Crack the eggs inside and top them with ground black pepper and dried oregano. Bake the meal at 355 degrees F for 20 minutes.
Per Serving: Calories 139; Fat 9.54g; Sodium 125mg; Carbs 1.35g; Fiber 0.4g; Sugar 0.34g; Protein 11.19g

Gorgeous Vanilla Granola

Prep Time: 5 minutes | Cook Time: 40 minutes | Serves: 4

1 cup rolled oats
3 tablespoons maple syrup
1 tablespoon coconut sugar
1 tablespoon neutral-flavored oil (such as refined coconut, sunflower, or safflower)
¼ teaspoon sea salt
¼ teaspoon cinnamon
¼ teaspoon vanilla

1. In a medium-size bowl, stir together the oats, maple syrup, coconut sugar, oil, salt, cinnamon, and vanilla until thoroughly combined. Transfer the mixture to a suitable baking pan. Place the Crisper Tray in the bottom position. 2. Place the pan on the tray and close the lid. Move SmartSwitch to AIR FRY/STOVETOP, and then use the center front arrows to select BAKE/ROAST. 3. Set the cooking temperature to 250 degrees F and the cooking time to 40 minutes. Stir the food every 10 minutes during cooking. 4. When cooked, store the dish in an airtight container once it's completely cooled and crisp. 5. The granola should keep for at least a week or two weeks in a cool, dry place.

Per Serving: Calories 136; Fat: 5.06g; Sodium: 148mg; Carbs: 27.79g; Fiber: 3.7g; Sugar: 11.4g; Protein: 4.08g

Strawberry Delight Parfait

Prep Time: 10 minutes | Cook Time: 40 minutes | Serves: 4

1 (12.3-ounce) package silken tofu, firm or extra-firm
2 pitted dates (optional)
¼ cup maple syrup
1 cup strawberries (fresh or frozen), plus 3 cups fresh strawberries, sliced
2 tablespoons neutral-flavored oil (such as refined coconut, sunflower, or safflower)
2 teaspoons vanilla
⅛ teaspoon sea salt

1. Make the granola and set aside. In a blender, place the tofu, dates (if using), and maple syrup, and blend them until smooth. 2. Add 1 cup of strawberries, the oil, vanilla, and salt, and blend them until velvety smooth. Set aside (this component can be refrigerated in an airtight container for about 7 days). 3. Place the Crisper Tray in the bottom position. Layer the parfaits on the tray and close the lid. Move SmartSwitch to AIR FRY/STOVETOP, and then use the center front arrows to select BAKE/ROAST. Set the cooking temperature to 250 degrees F and the cooking time to 40 minutes. 4. Enjoy immediately so as to preserve the crunch of the granola.

Per Serving: Calories 256; Fat: 13.05g; Sodium: 123mg; Carbs: 27.3g; Fiber: 2.4g; Sugar: 19.77g; Protein: 9.33g

Mung Bean "Quiche" with Sauce

Prep Time: 5 minutes | Cook Time: 15 minutes | Serves: 2

For the Lime Garlic Sauce
2 teaspoons tamari or shoyu
1 teaspoon fresh lime juice
1 large garlic clove, minced or pressed
Dash red chili flakes
For the "Quiche"
½ cup mung beans
½ cup water
¼ teaspoon sea salt
⅛ teaspoon freshly ground black pepper
½ cup minced onion
1 scallion, trimmed and chopped
Cooking oil spray (sunflower, safflower, or refined coconut)

1. Stir the tamari, lime juice, garlic, and chili flakesin a small bowl. Set aside. Soak the mung beans in plenty of water to cover overnight, or for about 8 hours. Drain the mung beans, rinse, and set them aside. 2. Place the soaked, drained beans in a blender with the water, salt, and pepper. Blend them until smooth. Stir in the onion and scallion, but do not blend. 3. Spray a suitable baking pan with a little oil spray and pour the batter into the oiled pan. Place the Crisper Tray in the bottom position. 4. Place the pan on the tray and close the lid. Move SmartSwitch to AIR FRY/STOVETOP, and then use the center front arrows to select BAKE/ROAST. 5. Set the cooking temperature to 390 degrees F and the cooking time to 15 minutes. 6. When cooked, a knife inserted in the center should come out clean. Cut the "quiche" into quarters and serve drizzled with the sauce.

Per Serving: Calories 33; Fat: 0.44g; Sodium: 626mg; Carbs: 6.55g; Fiber: 1.7g; Sugar: 2.64g; Protein: 1.98g

Scotch Eggs

Prep Time: 15 minutes | Cook Time: 20 minutes | Serves: 4

4 medium eggs, hard-boiled, peeled
2 cups ground pork
1 teaspoon dried basil
½ teaspoon salt
2 tablespoons almond flour

1. In the mixing bowl, mix ground pork with basil, salt, and almond flour. 2. Form 4 balls from the meat mixture. Fill every meatball with cooked egg. 3. Place the Crisper Tray in the bottom position. Place the meatballs on the tray and close the lid. Move SmartSwitch to AIR FRY/STOVETOP. Set the cooking temperature to 375 degrees F and the cooking time to 20 minutes. 4. Serve and enjoy.
Per Serving: Calories 281; Fat 20.7g; Sodium 401mg; Carbs 0.53g; Fiber 0.1g; Sugar 0.19g; Protein 21.54g

Easy Donut Holes

Prep Time: 15 minutes | Cook Time: 16 minutes | Serves: 6

1 tablespoon ground flaxseed
1½ tablespoons water
¼ cup nondairy milk, unsweetened
2 tablespoons neutral-flavored oil (sunflower, safflower, or refined coconut)
1½ teaspoons vanilla
1½ cups whole-wheat pastry flour or all-purpose gluten-free flour
¾ cup coconut sugar, divided
2½ teaspoons cinnamon, divided
½ teaspoon nutmeg
¼ teaspoon sea salt
¾ teaspoon baking powder
Cooking oil spray (refined coconut, sunflower, or safflower)

1. In a medium bowl, stir the flaxseed with the water and set aside for 5 minutes or until gooey and thick. Add the milk, oil, and vanilla. Stir them well and set this wet mixture aside. 2. In a small bowl, combine the flour, ½ cup coconut sugar, ½ teaspoon cinnamon, nutmeg, salt, and baking powder. Stir very well. Add this mixture to the wet mixture and stir together just until all of the ingredients are thoroughly combined. 3. Pull off bits of the dough and roll into balls (about 1-inch in size each). Place the Crisper Tray in the bottom position. Add the food to it, spray the food and close the lid. 4. Move SmartSwitch to AIR FRY/STOVETOP, set the cooking temperature to 350 degrees F and the cooking time to 16 minutes. 5. After 6 minutes of cooking time, spray the donut holes with oil again, flip them over, and spray them with oil again. Fry them for 2 more minutes, or until golden-brown. 6. During these last 2 minutes of frying, place the remaining 4 tablespoons coconut sugar and 2 teaspoons cinnamon in a bowl, and stir to combine. 7. When the donut holes are done frying, remove them one at a time and coat them as follows: Spray with oil again and toss with the cinnamon-sugar mixture. 8. Spray one last time, and coat with the cinnamon-sugar one last time. Enjoy fresh and warm if possible, as they're best that way.
Per Serving: Calories 245; Fat: 8.25g; Sodium: 104mg; Carbs: 38.7g; Fiber: 1.9g; Sugar: 13.01g; Protein: 3.93g

Garlic Potato Fries

Prep Time: 5 minutes | Cook Time: 16 minutes | Serves: 4

2 cups cubed potato (small cubes from 2 medium potatoes)
1½ teaspoons oil (olive or sunflower)
3 medium cloves garlic, minced or pressed
¼ teaspoon sea salt
¼ teaspoon onion granules
⅛ teaspoon freshly ground black pepper
Cooking oil spray (sunflower, safflower, or refined coconut)
½ tablespoon dried rosemary or fresh rosemary, minced

1. Toss the potatoes with the oil, garlic, salt, onion granules, and black pepper in a medium bowl. Stir them to evenly coat the potatoes with the seasonings. 2. Place the potatoes on the Crisper Tray and Roast them at 390 degrees F for 16 minutes, stirring them halfway through roasting. 3. When cooked, the potatoes should be tender and nicely browned. Add the potatoes back to the bowl and spray with oil. 4. Toss in the rosemary and enjoy.
Per Serving: Calories 84; Fat: 1.87g; Sodium: 152mg; Carbs: 15.52g; Fiber: 1.9g; Sugar: 1.65g; Protein: 1.84g

Churro Banana Oatmeal

Prep Time: 5 minutes | Cook Time: 10 minutes | Serves: 2

For the Churros
1 large yellow banana, peeled, cut in half lengthwise, then cut in half widthwise
2 tablespoons whole-wheat pastry flour
⅛ teaspoon sea salt
2 teaspoons oil (sunflower or melted coconut)
1 teaspoon water
Cooking oil spray (refined coconut, sunflower, or safflower)
1 tablespoon coconut sugar
½ teaspoon cinnamon
For the Oatmeal
¾ cup rolled oats
1½ cups water
Nondairy milk of your choice (optional)

1. Place the 4 banana pieces in a medium-size bowl and add the flour and salt; stir them gently. Add the oil and water, and stir them until evenly mixed. 2. Place the Crisper Tray in the bottom position. Add the food to it and close the lid. Move SmartSwitch to AIR FRY/STOVETOP, set the cooking temperature to 390 degrees F and the cooking time to 10 minutes. Turn the food halfway through cooking. 3. In a medium bowl, add the coconut sugar and cinnamon and stir to combine. When the banana pieces are nicely browned, spray with the oil and place in the cinnamon-sugar bowl. Toss gently with a spatula to coat the banana pieces with the mixture. 4. While the bananas are cooking, make your oatmeal. In a medium pot, bring the oats and water to a boil, and then reduce the heat to low. Simmer and stir them for 5 minutes or until all of the water is absorbed. 5. Place the oatmeal into two bowls. If desired, pour a small amount of nondairy milk on top (but not too much, or the banana pieces will get soggy when you add them). 6. Top your oatmeal with the coated banana pieces and serve immediately.
Per Serving: Calories 290; Fat: 14.2g; Sodium: 161mg; Carbs: 48.79g; Fiber: 8.3g; Sugar: 12.78g; Protein: 7.86g

Chia Banana Bread

Prep Time: 10 minutes | Cook Time: 25 minutes | Serves: 6

2 large bananas, very ripe, peeled
2 tablespoons neutral-flavored oil (sunflower or safflower)
2 tablespoons maple syrup
½ teaspoon vanilla
½ tablespoon chia seeds
½ tablespoon ground flaxseed
1 cup whole-wheat pastry flour
¼ cup coconut sugar
½ teaspoon cinnamon
¼ teaspoon salt
¼ teaspoon nutmeg
¼ teaspoon baking powder
¼ teaspoon baking soda
Cooking oil spray (sunflower, safflower, or refined coconut)

1. In a medium bowl, mash the peeled bananas with a fork until very mushy. Add the oil, maple syrup, vanilla, chia, and flaxseeds and stir well. 2. Add the flour, sugar, cinnamon, salt, nutmeg, baking powder, and baking soda, and stir just until thoroughly combined. 3. Pour the batter into a suitable baking pan, and smooth out the top. Place the Crisper Tray in the bottom position. Place the pan on the tray and close the lid. 4. Move SmartSwitch to AIR FRY/STOVETOP, and then use the center front arrows to select BAKE/ROAST. Set the cooking temperature to 350 degrees F and the cooking time to 25 minutes. 5. Bake the batter until a knife inserted in the center comes out clean. Let the dish cool for a minute or two, then cut into wedges and serve.
Per Serving: Calories 201; Fat: 6.36g; Sodium: 154mg; Carbs: 35g; Fiber: 4.5g; Sugar: 13.8g; Protein: 3.7g

Eggs with Chili Flakes

Prep Time: 5 minutes | Cook Time: 6 minutes | Serves: 4

5 eggs
1 teaspoon chili flakes
1 teaspoon avocado oil

1. Brush the Crisper Tray with avocado oil and crack the eggs inside. 2. Sprinkle the eggs with chili flakes and BAKE them at 360 degrees F for 6 minutes.
Per Serving: Calories 90; Fat 6.45g; Sodium 97mg; Carbs 0.73g; Fiber 0.2g; Sugar 0.25g; Protein 7g

Tasty Eggplant Spread

Prep Time: 15 minutes | Cook Time: 20 minutes | Serves: 4

3 eggplants
1 teaspoon chili flakes
1 teaspoon salt
½ teaspoon ground black pepper
2 tablespoons avocado oil

1. Peel the eggplants and rub them with salt. Place the Crisper Tray in the bottom position. 2. Add the food to it and close the lid. Move SmartSwitch to AIR FRY/STOVETOP, set the cooking temperature to 365 degrees F and the cooking time to 20 minutes. 3. Chop the eggplant after cooking and put it in the blender. Add all remaining ingredients and blend the mixture until smooth. 4. Serve and enjoy.

Per Serving: Calories 169; Fat 7.85g; Sodium 609mg; Carbs 25.03g; Fiber 12.6g; Sugar 14.84g; Protein 4.23g

Cheddar Broccoli Casserole

Prep Time: 10 minutes | Cook Time: 20 minutes | Serves: 4

2 cups broccoli, chopped
4 eggs, beaten
1 teaspoon chili flakes
½ cup Cheddar cheese, shredded
1 teaspoon avocado oil

1. Brush the cooking pot with avocado oil from inside. 2. Mix broccoli, eggs, chili flakes, and cheese in the mixing bowl. Place the mixture in the pot with the tray. Close the lid. 3. Move SmartSwitch to AIR FRY/STOVETOP, set the cooking temperature to 370 degrees F and the cooking time to 20 minutes.

Per Serving: Calories 213; Fat 16.54g; Sodium 234mg; Carbs 2.14g; Fiber 0.8g; Sugar 0.62g; Protein 13.66g

Coconut Cheese Mix

Prep Time: 10 minutes | Cook Time: 20 minutes | Serves: 6

1 cup of coconut milk
1 teaspoon avocado oil
2 tablespoons mascarpone
1 cup cheddar cheese, shredded
3 eggs, beaten

1. Brush the Crisper Tray with avocado oil. Mix coconut milk with mascarpone, cheese, and eggs. 2. Place the Crisper Tray in the bottom position. Add the ingredients to it and close the lid. 3. Move SmartSwitch to AIR FRY/STOVETOP, set the cooking temperature to 350 degrees F and the cooking time to 20 minutes.

Per Serving: Calories 152; Fat 11.61g; Sodium 190mg; Carbs 2.39g; Fiber 0g; Sugar 2.2g; Protein 9.33g

Deviled Eggs

Prep Time: 5 minutes | Cook Time: 15 minutes | Serves: 4

4 large eggs
1 cup ice cubes
1 cup water
2 tablespoons mayonnaise
1 teaspoon yellow mustard
½ teaspoon dill pickle juice
1 teaspoon finely diced sweet pickles
⅛ teaspoon salt
⅛ teaspoon ground black pepper
2 tablespoons finely grated Cheddar cheese
2 slices cooked bacon, crumbled

1. Add eggs to the Crisper Tray, and ROAST them at 250 degrees F for 15 minutes. Add ice and water to a medium bowl. 2. Transfer cooked eggs to this water bath immediately to stop cooking process. Let the eggs sit for 5 minutes, then carefully peel eggs. Cut eggs in half lengthwise. 3. Spoon yolks into a medium bowl. Arrange egg white halves on a medium plate. 4. Using a fork, blend egg yolks with mayonnaise, mustard, pickle juice, pickles, salt, and pepper. Fold in cheese. Spoon mixture into egg white halves. 5. Garnish with crumbled bacon and serve.

Per Serving: Calories 241; Fat: 17.52g; Sodium: 539mg; Carbs: 9.84g; Fiber: 1.9g; Sugar: 3.56g; Protein: 10.72g

Healthy Whole-Grain Corn Bread

Prep Time: 10 minutes | Cook Time: 25 minutes | Serves: 6

2 tablespoons ground flaxseed
3 tablespoons water
½ cup cornmeal
½ cup whole-wheat pastry flour
⅓ cup coconut sugar
½ tablespoon baking powder
¼ teaspoon sea salt
¼ teaspoon baking soda
½ tablespoon apple cider vinegar
½ cup plus 1 tablespoon nondairy milk (unsweetened)
¼ cup neutral-flavored oil (such as sunflower, safflower, or melted refined coconut)
Cooking oil spray (sunflower, safflower, or refined coconut)

1. In a small bowl, combine the flaxseed and water. Set aside for 5 minutes or until thick and gooey. In a medium bowl, add the cornmeal, flour, sugar, baking powder, salt, and baking soda. Combine thoroughly, stirring with a whisk. Set aside. 2. Add the vinegar, milk, and oil to the flaxseed mixture and stir them well. Add the wet mixture to the dry mixture and stir them gently just until thoroughly combined. 3. Pour the batter into a suitable baking pan. Place the Crisper Tray in the bottom position. Place the pan on the tray and close the lid. 4. Move SmartSwitch to AIR FRY/STOVETOP, and then use the center front arrows to select BAKE/ROAST. Set the cooking temperature to 350 degrees F and the cooking time to 25 minutes. 5. When done, the bread should be golden-browned and a knife inserted in the center comes out clean. Cut the dish into wedges and then top them with a little vegan margarine. 6. Enjoy.

Per Serving: Calories 136; Fat: 2.02g; Sodium: 166mg; Carbs: 26.95g; Fiber: 2.6g; Sugar: 7.78g; Protein: 3.63g

Savory Breakfast Cakes

Prep Time: 10 minutes | Cook Time: 40 minutes | Serves: 5

4 small potatoes (russet or Yukon Gold)
2 cups (lightly packed) kale, stems removed and finely chopped
1 cup chickpea flour
¼ cup nutritional yeast
¾ cup oat milk, plain and unsweetened (or your nondairy milk of choice)
2 tablespoons fresh lemon juice
2 teaspoons dried rosemary
2 teaspoons onion granules
1 teaspoon sea salt
½ teaspoon freshly ground black pepper
½ teaspoon turmeric powder
Cooking oil spray (sunflower, safflower, or refined coconut)

1. Scrub the potatoes, leaving the skins on for maximum nutrition. Place the Crisper Tray in the bottom position. Place the potatoes on the tray and close the lid. 2. Move SmartSwitch to AIR FRY/STOVETOP, and then use the center front arrows to select BAKE/ROAST. Set the cooking temperature to 390 degrees F and the cooking time to 30 minutes. 3. When the potatoes are cool enough to handle, chop the cooked potatoes into small pieces and place in a large bowl. Mash them with a potato masher or fork. 4. Add the kale, chickpea flour, yeast, milk, lemon, rosemary, onion granules, salt, pepper, and turmeric and stir them well until thoroughly combined. 5. Remove ¼ cup of batter and roll it into a ball with your hands. Smash it into a ½-inch thick patty (it will be about 3 inches in diameter) and place them on the tray. 6. Repeat with the remaining batter, taking care not to overlap the cakes. Bake them at the same cooking temperature for 10 minutes, spraying the tops with oil halfway through baking. 7. Serve plain or with the sauce of your choice. Leftover batter can be refrigerated in an airtight container for about 5 days.

Per Serving: Calories 405; Fat: 2.95g; Sodium: 997mg; Carbs: 81.57g; Fiber: 11.8g; Sugar: 13.47g; Protein: 17.01g

Olive Eggs

Prep Time: 5 minutes | Cook Time: 20 minutes | Serves: 4

4 eggs, beaten
2 Kalamata olives, sliced
1 teaspoon avocado oil
½ teaspoon ground paprika

1. Brush the Crisper Tray with avocado oil and pour the eggs inside. 2. Sprinkle the eggs with ground paprika and top with olives. Bake the meal at 360 degrees F for 20 minutes.

Per Serving: Calories 76; Fat 5.55g; Sodium 84mg; Carbs 0.53g; Fiber 0.1g; Sugar 0.2g; Protein 5.58g

Pork Sausage Patties

Prep Time: 10 minutes | Cook Time: 20 minutes | Serves: 4

12 ounces ground pork
¼ cup finely diced peeled yellow onion
1 teaspoon rubbed sage
1 tablespoon light brown sugar
⅛ teaspoon ground nutmeg
¼ teaspoon salt
¼ teaspoon ground black pepper
1 tablespoon water

1. Combine pork, onion, sage, brown sugar, nutmeg, salt, and pepper in a large bowl. 2. Form the mixture into eight patties. Place the Crisper Tray in the bottom position. Add the patties to it and close the lid. 3. Move SmartSwitch to AIR FRY/STOVETOP, set the cooking temperature to 350 degrees F and the cooking time to 10 minutes. 4. Flip the patties halfway through the cooking. You can cook the patties in batches. 5. Serve warm.
Per Serving: Calories 270; Fat: 18.31g; Sodium: 209mg; Carbs: 2.89g; Fiber: 0.2g; Sugar: 2.43g; Protein: 21.94g

Easy Hard "Boiled" Eggs

Prep Time: 5 minutes | Cook Time: 15 minutes | Serves: 8

8 large eggs, in shell
1 cup ice cubes
2 cups water

1. Add eggs to the Crisper Tray. Roast them at 250 degrees F for 15 minutes. Add ice and water to a large bowl. 2. Transfer cooked eggs to this water bath immediately to stop cooking process. 3. Let the eggs sit for 5 minutes, then peel and eat.
Per Serving: Calories 72; Fat: 4.76g; Sodium: 72mg; Carbs: 0.36g; Fiber: 0g; Sugar: 0.19g; Protein: 6.28g

Cheddar Coconut Biscuits

Prep Time: 15 minutes | Cook Time: 8 minutes | Serves: 4

½ cup coconut flour
¼ cup Cheddar cheese, shredded
1 egg, beaten
1 tablespoon cream cheese
1 tablespoon coconut oil, melted
¾ teaspoon baking powder
½ teaspoon ground cardamom

1. Mix all ingredients in the mixing bowl and knead the dough. Make 4 biscuits from the biscuits. Place the Crisper Tray in the bottom position. 2. Add the biscuits to it and close the lid. Move SmartSwitch to AIR FRY/STOVETOP, set the cooking temperature to 390 degrees F and the cooking time to 8 minutes. 3. Flip the biscuits from time to time to avoid burning. Serve warm.
Per Serving: Calories 114; Fat 8.39g; Sodium 118mg; Carbs 2.05g; Fiber 0.4g; Sugar 0.98g; Protein 3.88g

Brussels Sprouts with Eggs

Prep Time: 5 minutes | Cook Time: 20 minutes | Serves: 4

1 pound Brussels sprouts, shredded
8 eggs, beaten
1 teaspoon avocado oil
1 teaspoon ground turmeric
½ teaspoon salt

1. Mix all ingredients and stir them until homogenous. 2. Place the Crisper Tray in the bottom position. Add the ingredients to it and close the lid. Move SmartSwitch to AIR FRY/STOVETOP, set the cooking temperature to 365 degrees F and the cooking time to 20 minutes.
Pour the mixture in the Crisper Tray and cook at 365F for 20 minutes.
Per Serving: Calories 187; Fat 9.86g; Sodium 444mg; Carbs 11.29g; Fiber 4.5g; Sugar 2.84g; Protein 14.96g

Vegetable Tacos

Prep Time: 5 minutes | Cook Time: 12 minutes | Serves: 3

Cooking oil spray (sunflower, safflower, or refined coconut)
1 small zucchini
1 small-medium yellow onion
¼ teaspoon garlic granules
⅛ teaspoon sea salt
Freshly ground black pepper
1 (15-ounce) can vegan re-fried beans
6 corn tortillas
Fresh salsa of your choice
1 avocado, cut into slices, or fresh guacamole

1. Spray the Crisper Tray with the oil. Cut the zucchini and onion and place on the Crisper Tray. Spray with more oil and sprinkle evenly with the garlic, salt, and pepper to taste. 2. Move SmartSwitch to AIR FRY/STOVETOP, and then use the center front arrows to select BAKE/ROAST. Set the cooking temperature to 390 degrees F and the cooking time to 12 minutes, stirring them halfway through roasting. 3. When cooked, the vegetables should be nicely browned and tender. Warm the fried beans in a small pan over low heat by stirring them occasionally. Set aside. 4. To prepare the tortillas, sprinkle them individually with a little water, then place in a hot skillet, turning over as each side becomes hot. 5. To make the breakfast tacos: Place a corn tortilla on your plate and fill it with beans, roasted vegetables, salsa, and avocado slices.
Per Serving: Calories 271; Fat: 11.92g; Sodium: 744mg; Carbs: 39.98g; Fiber: 11.5g; Sugar: 6.02g; Protein: 6.93g

Chapter 2 Vegetable and Sides Recipes

Roasted Bell Peppers

Prep Time: 15 minutes | Cook Time: 15 minutes | Serves: 3

1 pound bell peppers, seeded and halved
1 chili pepper, seeded
2 tablespoons olive oil
Kosher salt and ground black pepper, to taste
1 teaspoon granulated garlic

1. Toss the peppers with the remaining ingredients. 2. Place the Crisper Tray in the bottom position. Add the food and close the lid. Move SmartSwitch to AIR FRY/STOVETOP, and then use the center front arrows to select BAKE/ROAST. Set the cooking temperature to 400 degrees F and the cooking time to 15 minutes. 3. Toss the food halfway through. Taste, adjust the seasonings and serve at room temperature. Bon appétit!

Per Serving: Calories 153; Fat 9.37g; Sodium 13mg; Carbs 17.45g; Fiber 2.7g; Sugar 9.25g; Protein 3.68g

Brown Mushrooms

Prep Time: 9 minutes | Cook Time: 7 minutes | Serves: 4

1 pound brown mushrooms, quartered
2 tablespoons sesame oil
1 tablespoon tamari sauce
1 garlic clove, pressed
Sea salt and ground black pepper, to taste

1. Toss the mushrooms with the remaining ingredients. Toss them until they are well coated on all sides. 2. Place the Crisper Tray in the bottom position. Add the food to it and close the lid. Move SmartSwitch to AIR FRY/STOVETOP, set the cooking temperature to 400 degrees F and the cooking time to 7 minutes. 3. Toss the food halfway through. Serve warm.

Per Serving: Calories 92; Fat 7.22g; Sodium 38mg; Carbs 5.31g; Fiber 1.4g; Sugar 3g; Protein 3.85g

Country-Style Vegetable Mix

Prep Time: 20 minutes | Cook Time: 15 minutes | Serves: 4

1 carrot, trimmed and sliced
1 parsnip, trimmed and sliced
1 celery stalk, trimmed and sliced
1 onion, peeled and diced
2 tablespoons olive oil
Sea salt and ground black pepper, to taste
1 teaspoon red pepper flakes, crushed

1. Toss all ingredients. Place the Crisper Tray in the bottom position. Add the food to it and close the lid. 2. Move SmartSwitch to AIR FRY/STOVETOP, set the cooking temperature to 380 degrees F and the cooking time to 15 minutes. 3. Toss the food halfway through. Bon appétit!

Per Serving: Calories 120; Fat 6.97g; Sodium 15mg; Carbs 14.36g; Fiber 2.5g; Sugar 6.77g; Protein 1.46g

Parmesan Zucchini Fritters

Prep Time: 45 minutes | Cook Time: 15 minutes | Serves: 4

1½ medium zucchini, trimmed and grated
½ teaspoon salt, divided
1 large egg, whisked
¼ teaspoon garlic powder
¼ cup grated Parmesan cheese

1. Place grated zucchini on a kitchen towel and sprinkle with ¼ teaspoon salt. Wrap in towel and let sit 30 minutes, then wring out as much excess moisture as possible. 2. Place zucchini into a large bowl and mix with egg, remaining salt, garlic powder, and Parmesan. Cut a piece of parchment to fit Crisper Tray. 3. Divide mixture into four mounds, about ⅓ cup each, and press out into 4" rounds on ungreased parchment. Place parchment with rounds into Crisper Tray. 4. Move SmartSwitch to AIR FRY/STOVETOP, set the cooking temperature to 400 degrees F and the cooking time to 12 minutes. 5. Flip the fritters halfway through. Fritters will be crispy on the edges and tender but firm in the center when done. 6. Serve warm.

Per Serving: Calories 241; Fat: 17.52g; Sodium: 539mg; Carbs: 9.84g; Fiber: 1.9g; Sugar: 3.56g; Protein: 10.72g

Chinese Corn on the Cob

Prep Time: 10 minutes | Cook Time: 6 minutes | Serves: 2

2 ears of corn, husked and halved
2 tablespoons Chinese chili oil
Sea salt and red pepper, to taste
2 tablespoons fresh cilantro, chopped

1. Toss the ears of corn with the oil, salt, and red pepper. 2. Place the Crisper Tray in the bottom position. Add the ears of corn to it and close the lid. Move SmartSwitch to AIR FRY/STOVETOP, set the cooking temperature to 390 degrees F and the cooking time to 6 minutes. 3. Toss them halfway through the cooking time. Garnish the ears of corn with the fresh cilantro. Enjoy!
Per Serving: Calories 253; Fat 15.37g; Sodium 109mg; Carbs 29.47g; Fiber 4.3g; Sugar 6.22g; Protein 4.96g

Cheese Broccoli Sticks

Prep Time: 10 minutes | Cook Time: 16 minutes | Serves: 2

1 (10-ounce) steamer bag broccoli florets, cooked according to package instructions
1 large egg
1 ounce Parmesan 100% cheese crisps, finely ground
½ cup shredded sharp Cheddar cheese
½ teaspoon salt
½ cup ranch dressing

1. Let cooked broccoli cool 5 minutes, then place into a food processor with egg, cheese crisps, Cheddar, and salt. Process on low for 30 seconds until all ingredients are combined and begin to stick together. 2. Cut a sheet of parchment paper to fit Crisper Tray. Take one scoop of mixture, about 3 tablespoons, and roll into a 4" stick shape, pressing down gently to flatten the top. 3. Place stick on ungreased parchment into Crisper Tray. Repeat with remaining mixture to form eight sticks. Move SmartSwitch to AIR FRY/STOVETOP, set the cooking temperature to 350 degrees F and the cooking time to 16 minutes. 4. Flip the sticks halfway through cooking. Sticks will be golden brown when done. 5. Serve warm with ranch dressing on the side for dipping.
Per Serving: Calories 241; Fat: 17.52g; Sodium: 539mg; Carbs: 9.84g; Fiber: 1.9g; Sugar: 3.56g; Protein: 10.72g

Broccoli Florets with Pepitas

Prep Time: 8 minutes | Cook Time: 6 minutes | Serves: 3

¾ pound broccoli florets
1½ tablespoons olive oil
1 teaspoon garlic powder
½ teaspoon onion powder
½ teaspoon mustard seeds
Sea salt and freshly ground black pepper, to taste
2 tablespoons pepitas, lightly roasted

1. Toss the broccoli with the olive oil, garlic powder, onion powder, mustard seeds, salt, and black pepper. 2. Place the Crisper Tray in the bottom position. Add the food to it and close the lid. Move SmartSwitch to AIR FRY/STOVETOP, set the cooking temperature to 395 degrees F and the cooking time to 6 minutes. 3. Flip the broccoli halfway through. Serve warm when done.
Per Serving: Calories 121; Fat 9.9g; Sodium 40mg; Carbs 5.61g; Fiber 3.8g; Sugar 0.57g; Protein 5.45g

Paprika Sweet Potatoes

Prep Time: 40 minutes | Cook Time: 35 minutes | Serves: 4

1 pound sweet potatoes, scrubbed and halved
3 tablespoons olive oil
1 teaspoon paprika
Sea salt and ground black pepper, to taste

1. Toss the sweet potatoes with the olive oil, paprika, salt, and black pepper. Place the Crisper Tray in the bottom position. 2. Add the food to it and close the lid. Move SmartSwitch to AIR FRY/STOVETOP, set the cooking temperature to 380 degrees F and the cooking time to 35 minutes. 3. Toss the food halfway through. Taste and adjust the seasonings. Bon appétit!
Per Serving: Calories 180; Fat 10.32g; Sodium 8mg; Carbs 20.49g; Fiber 2.8g; Sugar 0.95g; Protein 2.43g

Cheddar Cauliflower Pizza Crust

Prep Time: 20 minutes | Cook Time: 7 minutes | Serves: 2

1 (12-ounce) steamer bag cauliflower, cooked according to package instructions
½ cup shredded sharp Cheddar cheese
1 large egg
2 tablespoons blanched finely ground almond flour
1 teaspoon Italian seasoning

1. Let cooked cauliflower cool for 10 minutes. Using a kitchen towel, wring out excess moisture from cauliflower and place into food processor. 2. Add Cheddar, egg, flour, and Italian seasoning to processor and pulse ten times until cauliflower is smooth and all ingredients are combined. Divide cauliflower mixture into two equal portions and press each on the Crisper Tray. 3. Move SmartSwitch to AIR FRY/STOVETOP, set the cooking temperature to 360 degrees F and the cooking time to 7 minutes. Gently flip the crusts halfway through cooking. 4. Store crusts in refrigerator in an airtight container up to 4 days or freeze between sheets of parchment in a sealable storage bag for up to 2 months.
Per Serving: Calories 259; Fat: 18.96g; Sodium: 348mg; Carbs: 10.28g; Fiber: 5g; Sugar: 4.26g; Protein: 14.42g

Green Beans Salad

Prep Time: 10 minutes | Cook Time: 7 minutes | Serves: 3

¾ pound fresh green beans, washed and trimmed
2 tablespoons olive oil
½ cup green onions, thinly sliced
2 cups baby spinach
1 tablespoon fresh basil, chopped
1 green pepper, sliced
2 tablespoons fresh lemon juice
Sea salt and ground black pepper, to taste

1. Toss the green beans with 1 tablespoon of the olive oil. Place the Crisper Tray in the bottom position. 2. Add the green beans to it and close the lid. Move SmartSwitch to AIR FRY/STOVETOP, set the cooking temperature to 375 degrees F and the cooking time to 7 minutes. 3. Make sure to check the green beans halfway through the cooking time. 4. Add the green beans to a salad bowl; add in the remaining ingredients and stir to combine well. Enjoy!
Per Serving: Calories 123; Fat 9.74g; Sodium 21mg; Carbs 8.94g; Fiber 3.3g; Sugar 2.46g; Protein 2.4g

Parsnips Provencal

Prep Time: 15 minutes | Cook Time: 10 minutes | Serves: 4

1 pound parsnips, trimmed
1 tablespoon olive oil
1 teaspoon Herbs de province
1 teaspoon cayenne pepper
Sea salt and ground black pepper, to taste

1. Toss the parsnip with the olive oil and spices until they are well coated on all sides. 2. Place the Crisper Tray in the bottom position. Add the parsnip to it and close the lid. 3. Move SmartSwitch to AIR FRY/STOVETOP, set the cooking temperature to 380 degrees F and the cooking time to 10 minutes. 4. Toss the food halfway through. Serve and enjoy.
Per Serving: Calories 118; Fat 3.81g; Sodium 12mg; Carbs 21.03g; Fiber 5.8g; Sugar 5.49g; Protein 1.47g

Parsnip Burgers

Prep Time: 20 minutes | Cook Time: 15 minutes | Serves: 3

¾ pound peeled parsnips, shredded
¼ cup all-purpose flour
¼ cup cornflour
1 egg, lightly beaten
1 teaspoon cayenne pepper
Sea salt and ground black pepper, to taste

1. Mix all ingredients until everything is well combined. Form the mixture into three patties. 2. Place the Crisper Tray in the bottom position. Add the patties to it and close the lid. Move SmartSwitch to AIR FRY/STOVETOP, set the cooking temperature to 380 degrees F and the cooking time to 15 minutes. 3. Serve and enjoy.
Per Serving: Calories 183; Fat 2.34g; Sodium 33mg; Carbs 36.8g; Fiber 6.9g; Sugar 5.66g; Protein 5.11g

Butter Brussels Sprouts

Prep Time: 15 minutes | Cook Time: 10 minutes | Serves: 3

¾ pound Brussels sprouts, trimmed
1 tablespoon butter, melted
1 teaspoon red pepper flakes, crushed
Kosher salt and ground black pepper, to taste

1. Toss the Brussels sprouts with the butter and spices until they are well coated on all sides. 2. Place the Crisper Tray in the bottom position. Add the food to it and close the lid. Move SmartSwitch to AIR FRY/STOVETOP, set the cooking temperature to 380 degrees F and the cooking time to 10 minutes. 3. Toss the food halfway through. Serve warm and enjoy!
Per Serving: Calories 85; Fat 4.21g; Sodium 59mg; Carbs 10.7g; Fiber 4.5g; Sugar 2.55g; Protein 3.96g

Breaded Eggplant

Prep Time: 15 minutes | Cook Time: 15 minutes | Serves: 3

Sea salt and freshly ground black pepper, to taste
½ cup all-purpose flour
2 eggs
¾ pound eggplant, sliced
½ cup bread crumbs

1. In a shallow bowl, mix the salt, black pepper, and flour. 2. Whisk the eggs in the second bowl, and place the breadcrumbs in the third bowl. 3. Dip the eggplant slices in the flour mixture, then in the whisked eggs; finally, roll the eggplant slices over the breadcrumbs until they are well coated on all sides. 4. Place the Crisper Tray in the bottom position. Add the eggplant to it and close the lid. Move SmartSwitch to AIR FRY/STOVETOP, set the cooking temperature to 400 degrees F and the cooking time to 13 minutes. 5. Flip the food halfway through. Serve warm.
Per Serving: Calories 219; Fat 4.18g; Sodium 176mg; Carbs 36.22g; Fiber 5g; Sugar 5.29g; Protein 9.43g

Yummy Eggplant Rounds

Prep Time: 40 minutes | Cook Time: 10 minutes | Serves: 4

1 large eggplant, ends trimmed, cut into ½" slices
½ teaspoon salt
2 ounces Parmesan 100% cheese crisps, finely ground
½ teaspoon paprika
¼ teaspoon garlic powder
1 large egg

1. Sprinkle eggplant rounds with salt. Place rounds on a kitchen towel for 30 minutes to draw out excess water. Pat rounds dry. In a medium bowl, mix cheese crisps, paprika, and garlic powder. 2. In a separate medium bowl, whisk egg. Dip each eggplant round in egg, then gently press into cheese crisps to coat both sides. 3. Place eggplant rounds into the Crisper Tray. Move SmartSwitch to AIR FRY/STOVETOP, set the cooking temperature to 400 degrees F and the cooking time to 10 minutes. 4. Turn the food halfway through cooking. Eggplant will be golden and crispy when done. 5. Serve warm.
Per Serving: Calories 113; Fat: 5.42g; Sodium: 567mg; Carbs: 10.42g; Fiber: 4.2g; Sugar: 4.93g; Protein: 7.02g

Fried Portobello Mushrooms

Prep Time: 10 minutes | Cook Time: 7 minutes | Serves: 3

½ cup flour
2 eggs
1 cup seasoned breadcrumbs
1 teaspoon smoked paprika
Sea salt and ground black pepper, to taste
¾ pound Portobello mushrooms, sliced

1. Place the flour in a plate. Whisk the eggs in a shallow bowl. In a third bowl, mix the breadcrumbs, paprika, salt, and black pepper. 2. Dip your mushrooms in the flour, then dunk them in the whisked eggs, and finally toss them in the breadcrumb mixture. Toss until well coated on all sides. 3. Place the Crisper Tray in the bottom position. Add the mushrooms to it and close the lid. Move SmartSwitch to AIR FRY/STOVETOP, set the cooking temperature to 400 degrees F and the cooking time to 7 minutes. 4. Toss the food halfway through. Serve and enjoy.
Per Serving: Calories 346; Fat 7.41g; Sodium 3366mg; Carbs 48.96g; Fiber 9.6g; Sugar 8.08g; Protein 14.09g

Tomato Stuffed Peppers

Prep Time: 15 minutes | Cook Time: 15 minutes | Serves: 3

3 bell peppers, seeded and halved
1 tablespoon olive oil
1 small onion, chopped
2 garlic cloves, minced
Sea salt and ground black pepper, to taste
1 cup tomato sauce
2 ounces cheddar cheese, shredded

1. Toss the peppers with the oil. Mix the onion, garlic, salt, black pepper, and tomato sauce. Spoon the sauce into the pepper halves. 2. Place the Crisper Tray in the bottom position. Add the peppers to it and close the lid. Move SmartSwitch to AIR FRY/STOVETOP, set the cooking temperature to 400 degrees F and the cooking time to 15 minutes. 3. Top the peppers with the cheese after 10 minutes of cooking time. Serve and enjoy.

Per Serving: Calories 204; Fat 6.6g; Sodium 1431mg; Carbs 28.55g; Fiber 6.7g; Sugar 15g; Protein 6.39g

Caper Cauliflower Steaks

Prep Time: 5 minutes | Cook Time: 15 minutes | Serves: 4

1 small head cauliflower, leaves and core removed, cut into 4 (½"-thick) "steaks"
4 tablespoons olive oil, divided
1 medium lemon, zested and juiced, divided
¼ teaspoon salt
⅛ teaspoon ground black pepper
1 tablespoon salted butter, melted
1 tablespoon capers, rinsed

1. Brush each cauliflower "steak" with ½ tablespoon olive oil on both sides and sprinkle with lemon zest, salt, and pepper on both sides. Place cauliflower into the Crisper Tray. 2. Move SmartSwitch to AIR FRY/STOVETOP, set the cooking temperature to 400 degrees F and the cooking time to 15 minutes. 3. Turn cauliflower halfway through cooking. Steaks will be golden at the edges and browned when done. Transfer steaks to four medium plates. 4. In a small bowl, whisk remaining olive oil, butter, lemon juice, and capers, and pour evenly over steaks. 5. Serve warm.

Per Serving: Calories 156; Fat: 15.64g; Sodium: 232mg; Carbs: 4.37g; Fiber: 1.5g; Sugar: 1.65g; Protein: 1.41g

Warm Brussels Sprout

Prep Time: 5 minutes | Cook Time: 10 minutes | Serves: 3

¾ pound Brussels sprouts, trimmed
2 tablespoons olive oil
Sea salt and ground black pepper, to taste
½ teaspoon dried dill weed
1 tablespoon fresh lemon juice
1 tablespoon rice vinegar

1. Toss the Brussels sprouts with the olive oil and spices until they are well coated on all sides. 2. Place the Crisper Tray in the bottom position. Add the Brussels sprouts to it and close the lid. Move SmartSwitch to AIR FRY/STOVETOP, set the cooking temperature to 380 degrees F and the cooking time to 10 minutes. 3. Toss the food halfway through. Toss the Brussels sprouts with lemon juice and vinegar. Enjoy!

Per Serving: Calories 133; Fat 9.38g; Sodium 29mg; Carbs 11.13g; Fiber 4.5g; Sugar 2.65g; Protein 3.96g

Mini Sweet Pepper Nachos

Prep Time: 10 minutes | Cook Time: 5 minutes | Serves: 2

6 mini sweet peppers, seeded and sliced in half
¾ cup shredded Colby jack cheese
¼ cup sliced pickled jalapeños
½ medium avocado, peeled, pitted, and diced
2 tablespoons sour cream

1. Place peppers into a suitable nonstick baking dish. Sprinkle them with Colby and top with jalapeños. 2. Place dish into Crisper Tray. Adjust the temperature to 350 degrees F and set the timer for 5 minutes. 3. Cheese will be melted and bubbly when done. Remove dish from air fryer and top with avocado. 4. Drizzle with sour cream. Serve warm.

Per Serving: Calories 410; Fat: 23.04g; Sodium: 287mg; Carbs: 41.11; Fiber: 8.4g; Sugar: 0.58g; Protein: 17.24g

Easy Broccoli Salad

Prep Time: 8 minutes | Cook Time: 6 minutes | Serves: 3

¾ pound broccoli florets
¼ cup raw sunflower seeds
1 clove garlic, peeled and minced
1 small red onion, thinly sliced
¼ cup dried cranberries
¼ cup extra-virgin olive oil
2 tablespoons fresh lemon juice
1 tablespoon Dijon mustard
Sea salt and ground black pepper, to taste

1. Place the Crisper Tray in the bottom position. Add the broccoli florets to it and close the lid. Move SmartSwitch to AIR FRY/STOVETOP, set the cooking temperature to 395 degrees F and the cooking time to 6 minutes. 2. Toss the food halfway through. Toss the broccoli florets with the remaining ingredients. 3. Serve at room temperature.
Per Serving: Calories 192; Fat 14.57g; Sodium 252mg; Carbs 12.42g; Fiber 4.9g; Sugar 4.55g; Protein 6.72g

Cauliflower Florets with Parmesan

Prep Time: 15 minutes | Cook Time: 15 minutes | Serves: 4

1 pound cauliflower florets
2 tablespoons olive oil
1 teaspoon smoked paprika
Sea salt and ground black pepper, to taste
4 ounces parmesan cheese, grated

1. Toss the cauliflower florets with the olive oil and spices. Toss until they are well coated on all sides. 2. Place the Crisper Tray in the bottom position. Add the parsnip to it and close the lid. Move SmartSwitch to AIR FRY/STOVETOP, set the cooking temperature to 400 degrees F and the cooking time to 13 minutes. 3. Toss the food halfway through. Toss the warm cauliflower florets with cheese and enjoy.
Per Serving: Calories 210; Fat 15.05g; Sodium 546mg; Carbs 10.26g; Fiber 2.6g; Sugar 2.25g; Protein 10.38g

Parmesan Potatoes

Prep Time: 20 minutes | Cook Time: 15 minutes | Serves: 3

¾ pound potatoes, diced
1 tablespoon olive oil
1 teaspoon smoked paprika
1 teaspoon red pepper flakes, crushed
Sea salt and ground black pepper, to taste
2 ounces parmesan cheese, grated

1. Toss the potatoes with the olive oil and spices until well coated on all sides. 2. Place the Crisper Tray in the bottom position. Add the potatoes to it and close the lid. Move SmartSwitch to AIR FRY/STOVETOP, set the cooking temperature to 400 degrees F and the cooking time to 15 minutes. 3. Toss the food halfway through. Top the warm potatoes with cheese and serve immediately. Enjoy!
Per Serving: Calories 211; Fat 9.99g; Sodium 349mg; Carbs 23.41g; Fiber 3g; Sugar 1.03g; Protein 7.86g

Szechuan-Tasted Green Beans

Prep Time: 9 minutes | Cook Time: 7 minutes | Serves: 4

1 pound fresh green beans, trimmed
1 tablespoon sesame oil
½ teaspoon garlic powder
1 tablespoon soy sauce
Sea salt and Szechuan pepper, to taste
2 tablespoons sesame seeds, lightly toasted

1. Toss the green beans with the sesame oil and garlic powder. 2. Place the Crisper Tray in the bottom position. Add the green beans to it and close the lid. Move SmartSwitch to AIR FRY/STOVETOP, set the cooking temperature to 380 degrees F and the cooking time to 7 minutes. 3. Make sure to check the green beans halfway through the cooking time. 4. Toss the green beans with the remaining ingredients. Enjoy!
Per Serving: Calories 98; Fat 7.12g; Sodium 65mg; Carbs 7.71g; Fiber 2.9g; Sugar 2.26g; Protein 2.66g

Pan Pizza

Prep Time: 5 minutes | Cook Time: 10 minutes | Serves: 2

1 cup shredded mozzarella cheese
¼ medium red bell pepper, seeded and chopped
½ cup chopped fresh spinach leaves
2 tablespoons chopped black olives
2 tablespoons crumbled feta cheese

1. Sprinkle mozzarella into a suitable nonstick baking dish in an even layer. Add remaining ingredients on top. Place the dish on the Crisper Tray. 2. Move SmartSwitch to AIR FRY/STOVETOP, and then use the center front arrows to select BAKE/ROAST. Set the cooking temperature to 350 degrees F and the cooking time to 8 minutes. 3. Check the food halfway through cooking to avoid burning. Top of pizza will be golden brown and the cheese melted when done. 4. Remove dish from fryer and let cool 5 minutes before slicing and serving.

Per Serving: Calories 147; Fat: 4.37g; Sodium: 866mg; Carbs: 5.94g; Fiber: 2.5g; Sugar: 2.51g; Protein: 21.98g

Garlicky Vegetable Burgers

Prep Time: 10 minutes | Cook Time: 12 minutes | Serves: 4

8 ounces cremini mushrooms
2 large egg yolks
½ medium zucchini, trimmed and chopped
¼ cup peeled and chopped yellow onion
1 clove garlic, peeled and finely minced
½ teaspoon salt
¼ teaspoon ground black pepper

1. Place all ingredients into a food processor and pulse twenty times until finely chopped and combined. Separate mixture into four equal sections and press each into a burger shape. Place burgers into the Crisper Tray. 2. Move SmartSwitch to AIR FRY/STOVETOP, set the cooking temperature to 375 degrees F and the cooking time to 12 minutes. 3. Flip the burgers halfway through cooking. Burgers will be browned and firm when done. Place burgers on a large plate and let cool 5 minutes before serving.

Per Serving: Calories 205; Fat: 3.42g; Sodium: 303mg; Carbs: 44.03g; Fiber: 6.7g; Sugar: 1.69g; Protein: 6.97g

Spinach Artichoke-Stuffed Peppers

Prep Time: 10 minutes | Cook Time: 15 minutes | Serves: 4

2 ounces cream cheese, softened
½ cup shredded mozzarella cheese
½ cup chopped fresh spinach leaves
¼ cup chopped canned artichoke hearts
2 medium green bell peppers, halved and seeded

1. In a medium bowl, mix cream cheese, mozzarella, spinach, and artichokes. Spoon ¼ cheese mixture into each pepper half. Place the Crisper Tray in the bottom position. 2. Add the food to it and close the lid. Move SmartSwitch to AIR FRY/STOVETOP, set the cooking temperature to 320 degrees F and the cooking time to 15 minutes. 3. Peppers will be tender and cheese will be bubbling and brown when done. Serve warm.

Per Serving: Calories 82; Fat: 4.25g; Sodium: 189mg; Carbs: 5.19g; Fiber: 2.1g; Sugar: 2.08g; Protein: 6.95g

Cheese Spinach Frittata

Prep Time: 10 minutes | Cook Time: 20 minutes | Serves: 4

6 large eggs
½ cup heavy whipping cream
1 cup frozen chopped spinach, drained
1 cup shredded sharp Cheddar cheese
¼ cup peeled and diced yellow onion
½ teaspoon salt
¼ teaspoon ground black pepper

1. In a large bowl, whisk eggs and cream together. Whisk in spinach, Cheddar, onion, salt, and pepper. 2. Pour mixture into a suitable nonstick baking dish. Place dish on the Crisper Tray. 3. Bake the food at 320 degrees F for 20 minutes. Eggs will be firm and slightly browned when done. 4. Serve immediately.

Per Serving: Calories 313; Fat: 24.66g; Sodium: 645mg; Carbs: 3.73g; Fiber: 1.3g; Sugar: 1.43g; Protein: 19.18g

Pesto Veggies Skewers

Prep Time: 40 minutes | Cook Time: 8 minutes | Serves: 4

1 medium zucchini, trimmed and cut into ½" slices
½ medium yellow onion, peeled and cut into 1" squares
1 medium red bell pepper, seeded and cut into 1" squares
16 whole cremini mushrooms
⅓ cup basil pesto
½ teaspoon salt
¼ teaspoon ground black pepper

1. Divide zucchini slices, onion, and bell pepper into eight even portions. Place on 6" skewers for a total of eight kebabs. 2 Add 2 mushrooms to each skewer and brush kebabs generously with pesto. Sprinkle each kebab with salt and black pepper or all sides, then place into the Crisper Tray. 3. Move SmartSwitch to AIR FRY/STOVETOP, set the cooking temperature to 375 degrees F and the cooking time to 8 minutes. 4. Turn the kebabs halfway through cooking. Vegetables will be browned at the edges and tender-crisp when done. 5. Serve warm.
Per Serving: Calories 60; Fat: 0.27g; Sodium: 295mg; Carbs: 14.34g; Fiber: 2.6g; Sugar: 2.3g; Protein: 2.02g

Cauliflower Rice-Stuffed Bell Peppers

Prep Time: 10 minutes | Cook Time: 15 minutes | Serves: 4

2 cups uncooked cauliflower rice
¾ cup drained canned petite diced tomatoes
2 tablespoons olive oil
1 cup shredded mozzarella cheese
¼ teaspoon salt
¼ teaspoon ground black pepper
4 medium green bell peppers, tops removed, seeded

1. In a large bowl, mix all ingredients except bell peppers. Scoop mixture evenly into peppers. Place peppers into the Crisper Tray. 2. Move SmartSwitch to AIR FRY/STOVETOP, set the cooking temperature to 350 degrees F and the cooking time to 15 minutes. 3. Peppers will be tender and cheese will be melted when done. Serve warm.
Per Serving: Calories 139; Fat: 7.11g; Sodium: 427mg; Carbs: 9.73g; Fiber: 3.2g; Sugar: 5.03g; Protein: 11.29g

Stuffed Mushrooms

Prep Time: 10 minutes | Cook Time: 8 minutes | Serves: 4

3 ounces cream cheese, softened
½ medium zucchini, trimmed and chopped
¼ cup seeded and chopped red bell pepper
1½ cups chopped fresh spinach leaves
4 large portobello mushrooms, stems removed
2 tablespoons coconut oil, melted
½ teaspoon salt

1. In a medium bowl, mix cream cheese, zucchini, pepper, and spinach. Drizzle mushrooms with coconut oil and sprinkle with salt. 2. Scoop ¼ zucchini mixture into each mushroom. Place mushrooms into the Crisper Tray. Move SmartSwitch to AIR FRY/STOVETOP, set the cooking temperature to 400 degrees F and the cooking time to 8 minutes. 3. Portobellos will be tender and tops will be browned when done. Serve warm.
Per Serving: Calories 145; Fat: 13.31g; Sodium: 428mg; Carbs: 4.27g; Fiber: 2g; Sugar: 1.72g; Protein: 4.44g

Carrot Sticks with Sesame Seeds

Prep Time: 20 minutes | Cook Time: 15 minutes | Serves: 3

¾ pound carrots, trimmed and cut into sticks
2 tablespoons butter, melted
Coarse sea salt and white pepper, to taste
1 tablespoon sesame seeds, lightly toasted

1. Toss the carrots with the butter, salt, and white pepper. 2. Place the Crisper Tray in the bottom position. Add the carrots to it and close the lid. Move SmartSwitch to AIR FRY/STOVETOP, set the cooking temperature to 380 degrees F and the cooking time to 15 minutes. 3. Make sure to check the carrots halfway through the cooking time. Top the carrots with the sesame seeds. Bon appétit!
Per Serving: Calories 130; Fat 9.54g; Sodium 129mg; Carbs 11.06g; Fiber 3.9g; Sugar 4.7g; Protein 1.79g

Eggplant Stacks with Alfredo Sauce

Prep Time: 5 minutes | Cook Time: 15 minutes | Serves: 6

1 large eggplant, ends trimmed, cut into ¼" slices
1 medium beefsteak tomato, cored and cut into ¼" slices
1 cup Alfredo sauce
8 ounces fresh mozzarella cheese, cut into 18 slices
2 tablespoons fresh parsley leaves

1. Place 6 slices eggplant in bottom of a suitable nonstick baking dish. Place 1 slice tomato on top of each eggplant round, followed by 1 tablespoon Alfredo and 1 slice mozzarella. 2. Repeat with remaining ingredients, about three repetitions. Cover dish with aluminum foil and place dish on the Crisper Tray. 3. Roast the food at 350 degrees F for 12 minutes. Eggplant will be tender when done. Sprinkle parsley evenly over each stack. 4. Serve warm.

Per Serving: Calories 90; Fat: 0.25g; Sodium: 589mg; Carbs: 9.78g; Fiber: 4.3g; Sugar: 5.57g; Protein: 13.6g

Parmesan Eggplant Pieces

Prep Time: 40 minutes | Cook Time: 17 minutes | Serves: 4

1 medium eggplant, ends trimmed, sliced into ½" rounds
¼ teaspoon salt
2 tablespoons coconut oil
½ cup grated Parmesan cheese
1 ounce 100% cheese crisps, finely crushed
½ cup low-carb marinara sauce
½ cup shredded mozzarella cheese

1. Sprinkle eggplant rounds with salt on both sides and wrap in a kitchen towel for 30 minutes. Press to remove excess water, then drizzle rounds with coconut oil on both sides. 2. In a medium bowl, mix Parmesan and cheese crisps. Press each eggplant slice into mixture to coat both sides. Place rounds on the Crisper Tray. 3. Move SmartSwitch to AIR FRY/STOVETOP, set the cooking temperature to 350 degrees F and the cooking time to 15 minutes. 4. Flip the rounds halfway through cooking. When done, the rounds should be crispy around the edges, Spoon marinara over rounds and sprinkle with mozzarella. 5. Continue cooking them for an additional 2 minutes until cheese is melted. Serve warm.

Per Serving: Calories 241; Fat: 17.52g; Sodium: 539mg; Carbs: 9.84g; Fiber: 1.9g; Sugar: 3.56g; Protein: 10.72g

White Cheddar Mushroom Soufflés

Prep Time: 15 minutes | Cook Time: 15 minutes | Serves: 4

3 large eggs, whites and yolks separated
½ cup sharp white Cheddar cheese
3 ounces cream cheese, softened
¼ teaspoon cream of tartar
¼ teaspoon salt
¼ teaspoon ground black pepper
½ cup cremini mushrooms, sliced

1. In a large bowl, whip egg whites until stiff peaks form, about 2 minutes. In a separate large bowl, beat Cheddar, egg yolks, cream cheese, cream of tartar, salt, and pepper together until combined. 2. Fold egg whites into cheese mixture, being careful not to stir. Fold in mushrooms, then pour mixture evenly into four ungreased 4" ramekins. Place ramekins on the Crisper Tray. 3. Bake the food at 350 degrees F for 12 minutes. Eggs will be browned on the top and firm in the center when done. 4. Serve warm.

Per Serving: Calories 185; Fat: 15.24g; Sodium: 398mg; Carbs: 1.65g; Fiber: 0.1g; Sugar: 1.09g; Protein: 10.27g

Spicy Potatoes

Prep Time: 20 minutes | Cook Time: 15 minutes | Serves: 4

1 pound potatoes, diced into bite-sized chunks
1 tablespoon olive oil
Sea salt and ground black pepper, to taste
1 teaspoon chili powder

1. Toss the potatoes with the remaining ingredients until well coated on all sides. 2. Place the Crisper Tray in the bottom position. Add the food to it and close the lid. Move SmartSwitch to AIR FRY/STOVETOP, set the cooking temperature to 400 degrees F and the cooking time to 13 minutes. 3. Flip halfway through.

Per Serving: Calories 124; Fat 3.6g; Sodium 27mg; Carbs 21.21g; Fiber 2.9g; Sugar 1.51g; Protein 2.61g

Spinach Flatbread

Prep Time: 10 minutes | Cook Time: 10 minutes | Serves: 4

1 cup blanched finely ground almond flour
2 ounces cream cheese
2 cups shredded mozzarella cheese
1 cup chopped fresh spinach leaves
2 tablespoons basil pesto

1. Place flour, cream cheese, and mozzarella in a large microwave-safe bowl and microwave on high 45 seconds, then stir. Fold in spinach and microwave an additional 15 seconds. Stir until a soft dough ball forms. 2. Cut two pieces of parchment paper to fit Crisper Tray. Separate dough into two sections and press each out on ungreased parchment. 3. Spread 1 tablespoon pesto over each flatbread and place rounds on parchment into the Crisper Tray. Move SmartSwitch to AIR FRY/STOVETOP, set the cooking temperature to 350 degrees F and the cooking time to 8 minutes. 4. Flip the crusts after 4 minutes of cooking time. Flatbread will be golden when done. Let the dish cool 5 minutes before slicing and serving.
Per Serving: Calories 241; Fat: 17.52g; Sodium: 539mg; Carbs: 9.84g; Fiber: 1.9g; Sugar: 3.56g; Protein: 10.72g

Savory Cloud Eggs

Prep Time: 5 minutes | Cook Time: 10 minutes | Serves: 2

2 large eggs, whites and yolks separated
¼ teaspoon salt
¼ teaspoon dried oregano
2 tablespoons chopped fresh chives
2 teaspoons salted butter, melted

1. In a large bowl, whip egg whites until stiff peaks form, about 3 minutes. Place egg whites evenly into two ungreased ramekins. Sprinkle them evenly with salt, oregano, and chives. 2. Place 1 whole egg yolk in center of each ramekin and drizzle with butter. Place ramekins into Crisper Tray. 3. Bake the ramekins at 350 degrees F for 8 minutes. Egg whites will be fluffy and browned when done. 4. Serve warm.
Per Serving: Calories 241; Fat: 17.52g; Sodium: 539mg; Carbs: 9.84g; Fiber: 1.9g; Sugar: 3.56g; Protein: 10.72g

Crispy Cabbage Steaks with Parsley

Prep Time: 5 minutes | Cook Time: 10 minutes | Serves: 4

1 small head green cabbage, cored and cut into ½"-thick slices
¼ teaspoon salt
¼ teaspoon ground black pepper
2 tablespoons olive oil
1 clove garlic, peeled and finely minced
½ teaspoon dried thyme
½ teaspoon dried parsley

1. Sprinkle each side of cabbage with salt and pepper, then place into the Crisper Tray, working in batches if needed. Drizzle each side of cabbage with olive oil, then sprinkle with remaining ingredients on both sides. 2. Move SmartSwitch to AIR FRY/STOVETOP, set the cooking temperature to 350 degrees F and the cooking time to 10 minutes. 3. Flip the food halfway through cooking. Cabbage will be browned at the edges and tender when done. 4. Serve warm.
Per Serving: Calories 241; Fat: 17.52g; Sodium: 539mg; Carbs: 9.84g; Fiber: 1.9g; Sugar: 3.56g; Protein: 10.72g

Spaghetti Squash

Prep Time: 10 minutes | Cook Time: 45 minutes | Serves: 6

1 (4-pound) spaghetti squash, halved and seeded
2 tablespoons coconut oil
4 tablespoons salted butter, melted
1 teaspoon garlic powder
2 teaspoons dried parsley

1. Brush shell of spaghetti squash with coconut oil. Brush inside with butter. Sprinkle inside with garlic powder and parsley. Place squash skin side down into the Crisper Tray, working in batches if needed. 2. Move SmartSwitch to AIR FRY/STOVETOP, set the cooking temperature to 350 degrees F and the cooking time to 45 minutes. 3. Flip squash after 30 minutes of cooking time. Use a fork to remove spaghetti strands from shell and serve warm.
Per Serving: Calories 115; Fat: 9.7g; Sodium: 44mg; Carbs: 7.89g; Fiber: 1.1g; Sugar: 0.02g; Protein: 0.73g

Chapter 3 Poultry Recipes

Healthy Chicken Fingers

Prep Time: 20 minutes | Cook Time: 12 minutes | Serves: 4

1 egg, whisked
½ cup all-purpose flour
1 teaspoon garlic powder
1 teaspoon cayenne pepper
Sea salt and ground black pepper, to taste
¼ cup breadcrumbs
¼ cup parmesan cheese, grated
1½ pounds chicken breast boneless, skinless and cut into strips

1. Mix the egg and flour in a shallow bowl. 2. In a separate bowl, whisk the garlic powder, cayenne pepper, salt, black pepper, breadcrumbs, and parmesan cheese. 3. Dip the chicken breasts into the egg mixture. Roll the chicken breasts over the breadcrumb mixture. Place the Crisper Tray in the bottom position. 4. Add the chicken to it and close the lid. Move SmartSwitch to AIR FRY/STOVETOP, set the cooking temperature to 380 degrees F and the cooking time to 12 minutes. 5. Flip the food halfway through. Serve and enjoy.
Per Serving: Calories 338; Fat 7.86g; Sodium 256mg; Carbs 19.61g; Fiber 1.1g; Sugar 1.14g; Protein 44.35g

Breaded Chicken Breasts

Prep Time: 15 minutes | Cook Time: 12 minutes | Serves: 4

1 pound chicken breasts, boneless and skinless
1 tablespoon butter, room temperature
1 egg, whisked
1 teaspoon cayenne pepper
1 teaspoon garlic powder
Kosher salt and ground black pepper, to taste
½ cup breadcrumbs

1. Pat the chicken dry with paper towels. In a bowl, thoroughly combine the butter, egg, cayenne pepper, garlic powder, kosher salt, black pepper. 2. Dip the chicken breasts into the egg mixture. Roll the chicken breasts over the breadcrumbs. 3. Place the Crisper Tray in the bottom position. Add the chicken to it and close the lid. Move SmartSwitch to AIR FRY/STOVETOP, set the cooking temperature to 380 degrees F and the cooking time to 12 minutes. 4. Flip the food halfway through. Serve and enjoy.
Per Serving: Calories 298; Fat 15.24g; Sodium 210mg; Carbs 11.68g; Fiber 1g; Sugar1.52g; Protein 27.27g

Bone-in Chicken Wings

Prep Time: 25 minutes | Cook Time: 22 minutes | Serves: 3

1 pound chicken wings, bone-in
Sea salt and red pepper flakes, to taste
2 tablespoons olive oil
½ cup parmesan cheese, grated
2 cloves garlic, pressed

1. Pat the chicken dry with kitchen towels. Toss the chicken breasts with the remaining ingredients. 2. Place the Crisper Tray in the bottom position. Add the chicken to it and close the lid. 3. Move SmartSwitch to AIR FRY/STOVETOP, set the cooking temperature to 380 degrees F and the cooking time to 22 minutes. 4. Flip the food halfway through. Serve and enjoy.
Per Serving: Calories 349; Fat 19.05g; Sodium 482mg; Carbs 4.47g; Fiber 0.3g; Sugar 1.1g; Protein 38.31g

Palatable Chicken Drumsticks

Prep Time: 5 minutes | Cook Time: 20 minutes | Serves: 3

3 chicken drumsticks, bone-in
Kosher salt and ground black pepper, to taste
2 tablespoons olive oil
2 tablespoons soy sauce
1 tablespoon rice vinegar
1 teaspoon garlic powder

1. Pat the chicken drumsticks dry with paper towels. Toss the chicken drumsticks with the remaining ingredients. 2. Place the Crisper Tray in the bottom position. Add the chicken to it and close the lid. Move SmartSwitch to AIR FRY/STOVETOP, set the cooking temperature to 370 degrees F and the cooking time to 20 minutes. 3. Flip the food halfway through. Serve and enjoy.
Per Serving: Calories 326; Fat 22.91g; Sodium 300mg; Carbs 4.07g; Fiber 0.5g; Sugar 2.1g; Protein 24.51g

Savory Turkey Breasts

Prep Time: 65 minutes | Cook Time: 20 minutes | Serves: 5

2 tablespoons olive oil
Sea salt and freshly cracked black pepper, to taste
1 tablespoon Dijon mustard
1 tablespoon hot sauce
1 teaspoon smoked paprika
1 teaspoon dried basil
1 teaspoon dried thyme
2 pounds turkey breast, bone-in

1. In a mixing bowl, thoroughly combine the olive oil, salt, black pepper, mustard, hot sauce, paprika, basil, and thyme. 2. Rub the mixture all over the turkey breast. Place the Crisper Tray in the bottom position. 3. Add the turkey breast to it and close the lid. Move SmartSwitch to AIR FRY/STOVETOP, set the cooking temperature to 380 degrees F and the cooking time to 60 minutes. 4. Flip the food every 20 minutes. Serve and enjoy.
Per Serving: Calories 337; Fat 18.32g; Sodium 167mg; Carbs 0.79g; Fiber 0.4g; Sugar 0.22g; Protein 40g

Seasoned Turkey Drumettes

Prep Time: 50 minutes | Cook Time: 40 minutes | Serves: 4

1½ pounds turkey drumettes
1 tablespoon sesame oil
1 teaspoon poultry seasoning mix
Sea salt and ground black pepper, to taste

1. Toss the turkey drumettes with the remaining ingredients. Place the Crisper Tray in the bottom position. 2. Add the turkey drumettes to it and close the lid. Move SmartSwitch to AIR FRY/STOVETOP, set the cooking temperature to 400 degrees F and the cooking time to 40 minutes. 3. Flip the food halfway through. Let the turkey rest for 10 minutes before carving and serving. 4. Serve and enjoy.
Per Serving: Calories 853; Fat 79.06g; Sodium 75mg; Carbs 0.61g; Fiber 0.2g; Sugar 0.01g; Protein 32.47g

Rustic Duck Fillet

Prep Time: 10 minutes | Cook Time: 30 minutes | Serves: 4

1½ pounds duck fillet
1 tablespoon honey
2 tablespoons dark soy sauce
1 tablespoon soybean paste

1. Toss the duck fillets with the remaining ingredients. 2. Place the Crisper Tray in the bottom position. Add the duck fillets to it and close the lid. 3. Move SmartSwitch to AIR FRY/STOVETOP, set the cooking temperature to 330 degrees F and the cooking time to 15 minutes. 4. Flip the food halfway through. Turn the heat to 350 degrees F and continue to cook for about 15 minutes or until cooked through. 5. Let it rest for 10 minutes before carving and serving.
Per Serving: Calories 404; Fat 27.57g; Sodium 216mg; Carbs 6.75g; Fiber 0.3g; Sugar 5.85g; Protein 30.73g

Chili Chicken Drumsticks

Prep Time: 10 minutes | Cook Time: 20 minutes | Serves: 6

6 chicken drumsticks
1 teaspoon dried oregano
1 tablespoon lemon juice
½ teaspoon lemon zest, grated
1 tablespoon avocado oil
1 teaspoon ground cumin
½ teaspoon chili flakes
1 teaspoon garlic powder
½ teaspoon ground coriander

1. Rub the chicken drumsticks with dried oregano, lemon juice, lemon zest, ground cumin, chili flakes, garlic powder, and ground coriander. Then sprinkle them with avocado oil. 2. Transfer the food to the Crisper Tray. Move SmartSwitch to AIR FRY/STOVETOP, set the cooking temperature to 375 degrees F and the cooking time to 20 minutes. 3. Serve warm.
Per Serving: Calories 241; Fat: 17.52g; Sodium: 539mg; Carbs: 9.84g; Fiber: 1.9g; Sugar: 3.56g; Protein: 10.72g calories 85, fat 3.1, fiber 0.3, carbs 0.9, protein 12.9

Dill Chicken with Parmesan

Prep Time: 15 minutes | Cook Time: 20 minutes | Serves: 6

18 oz. chicken breast, skinless, boneless
5 oz. pork rinds
3 oz. Parmesan, grated
3 eggs, beaten
1 teaspoon chili flakes
1 teaspoon ground paprika
2 tablespoons avocado oil
1 teaspoon Erythritol
¼ teaspoon onion powder
1 teaspoon cayenne pepper
1 chili pepper, minced
½ teaspoon dried dill

1. In the shallow bowl mix up chili flakes, ground paprika, Erythritol. Onion powder, and cayenne pepper. Add dried dill and stir the mixture gently. Then rub the chicken breast in the spice mixture. 2. Then rub the chicken with minced chili pepper. Dip the chicken breast in the beaten eggs. 3. After this, coat it in the Parmesan and dip in the eggs again. Then coat the chicken in the pork rinds and sprinkle with avocado oil. 4. Preheat the air fryer to 380F. Put the chicken breast in the air fryer and cook it for 16 minutes. Then flip the chicken breast on another side and cook it for 4 minutes more.
Per Serving: Calories 241; Fat: 17.52g; Sodium: 539mg; Carbs: 9.84g; Fiber: 1.9g; Sugar: 3.56g; Protein: 10.72g calories 318, fat 16.5, fiber 0.5, carbs 1.5, protein 40.7

Hoisin Chicken Drumsticks

Prep Time: 25 minutes | Cook Time: 25 minutes | Serves: 4

½ teaspoon hoisin sauce
½ teaspoon salt
½ teaspoon chili powder
½ teaspoon ground black pepper
½ teaspoon ground cumin
¼ teaspoon xanthan gum
1 teaspoon apple cider vinegar
1 tablespoon sesame oil
3 tablespoons coconut cream
½ teaspoon minced garlic
½ teaspoon chili paste
1 pound chicken drumsticks
2 tablespoons almond flour

1. Rub the chicken drumsticks with salt, chili powder, ground black pepper, ground cumin, and leave for 10 minutes to marinate. 2. Meanwhile, in the mixing bowl mix up chili paste, minced garlic, coconut cream, apple cider vinegar, xanthan gum, and almond flour. 3. Coat the chicken drumsticks in the coconut cream mixture well, and leave to marinate for 10 minutes more. Transfer the food to the Crisper Tray. 4. Move SmartSwitch to AIR FRY/STOVETOP, set the cooking temperature to 375 degrees F and the cooking time to 22 minutes. 5. Serve hot.
Per Serving: Calories 241; Fat: 17.52g; Sodium: 539mg; Carbs: 9.84g; Fiber: 1.9g; Sugar: 3.56g; Protein: 10.72g calories 279, fat 14.5, fiber 1.7, carbs 3.4, protein 32.4

Truvia Chicken Mix

Prep Time: 15 minutes | Cook Time: 16 minutes | Serves: 4

1 pound chicken wings
¼ cup cream cheese
1 tablespoon apple cider vinegar
1 teaspoon Truvia
½ teaspoon smoked paprika
½ teaspoon ground nutmeg
1 teaspoon avocado oil

1. In the mixing bowl mix up cream cheese, Truvia, apple cider vinegar, smoked paprika, and ground nutmeg. Then add the chicken wings and coat them in the cream cheese mixture well. 2. Leave the chicken winds in the cream cheese mixture for 10-15 minutes to marinate. Transfer the chicken wings to the Crisper Tray. 3. Move SmartSwitch to AIR FRY/STOVETOP, set the cooking temperature to 380 degrees F and the cooking time to 16 minutes. 4. Flip the chicken wings and brush them with the cream cheese marinade halfway through cooking. 5. Serve warm.
Per Serving: Calories 241; Fat: 17.52g; Sodium: 539mg; Carbs: 9.84g; Fiber: 1.9g; Sugar: 3.56g; Protein: 10.72g calories 271, fat 13.7, fiber 0.2, carbs 1.2, protein 34

Greek Chicken Salad

Prep Time: 20 minutes | Cook Time: 12 minutes | Serves: 4

1 pound chicken breasts, boneless, skinless
1 red onion, thinly sliced
1 bell pepper, sliced
4 Kalamata olives, pitted and minced
1 small Greek cucumber, grated and squeezed
4 tablespoons Greek yogurt
4 tablespoons mayonnaise
1 tablespoon fresh lemon juice
Coarse sea salt and red pepper flakes, to taste

1. Pat the chicken dry with paper towels. Place the Crisper Tray in the bottom position. 2. Add the chicken to it and close the lid. Move SmartSwitch to AIR FRY/STOVETOP, set the cooking temperature to 380 degrees F and the cooking time to 12 minutes. 3. Flip the food halfway through. Chop the chicken breasts and transfer it to a salad bowl; add in the remaining ingredients and toss to combine well. 4. Enjoy.
Per Serving: Calories 272; Fat 16.29g; Sodium 239mg; Carbs 4.73g; Fiber 0.9g; Sugar 2.74g; Protein 25.82g

Chicken Muffin Sandwiches

Prep Time: 20 minutes | Cook Time: 12 minutes | Serves: 4

1 pound chicken breasts
1 tablespoon olive oil
Sea salt and black pepper, to taste
4 slices cheddar cheese
4 teaspoons yellow mustard
4 English muffins, lightly toasted

1. Pat the chicken dry with kitchen towels. Toss the chicken breasts with the olive oil, salt, and pepper. 2. Place the Crisper Tray in the bottom position. Add the chicken to it and close the lid. 3. Move SmartSwitch to AIR FRY/STOVETOP, set the cooking temperature to 380 degrees F and the cooking time to 12 minutes. 4. Flip the food halfway through. Shred the chicken using two forks and serve with cheese, mustard, and English muffins. Enjoy.
Per Serving: Calories 473; Fat 24.66g; Sodium 509mg; Carbs 6g; Fiber 27.26g; Sugar 1.59g; Protein 35.75g

Bacon Stuffed Chicken Breasts

Prep Time: 25 minutes | Cook Time: 20 minutes | Serves: 4

1 pound chicken breasts
4 tablespoons goat cheese
4 tablespoons bacon
1 tablespoon olive oil
½ teaspoon garlic powder
1 teaspoon dried basil
1 teaspoon dried oregano
1 teaspoon dried parsley flakes

1. Flatten the chicken breasts with a mallet. Stuff each piece of chicken with cheese and bacon. Roll them up and secure with toothpicks. 2. Sprinkle the chicken with olive oil, garlic powder, basil, oregano, and parsley. 3. Place the Crisper Tray in the bottom position. Add the chicken to it and close the lid. Move SmartSwitch to AIR FRY/STOVETOP, set the cooking temperature to 400 degrees F and the cooking time to 20 minutes. 4. Turn the chicken over halfway through. 5. Serve and enjoy.
Per Serving: Calories 300; Fat 19.78g; Sodium 452mg; Carbs 2.47g; Fiber 0.5g; Sugar 1.14g; Protein 27.25g

Garlicky Chicken Wings

Prep Time: 10 minutes | Cook Time: 30 minutes | Serves: 4

2 pounds chicken wings
¼ cup olive oil
Juice of 2 lemons
Zest of 1 lemon, grated
A pinch of salt and black pepper
2 garlic cloves, minced

1. In a bowl, mix the chicken wings with the rest of the ingredients and toss well. Put the chicken wings in your air fryer's basket and cook at 400 degrees F for 30 minutes, shaking halfway. 2. Divide between plates and serve with a side salad.
Per Serving: Calories 241; Fat: 17.52g; Sodium: 539mg; Carbs: 9.84g; Fiber: 1.9g; Sugar: 3.56g; Protein: 10.72g calories 263, fat 14, fiber 4, carbs 6, protein 15

Greek Chicken Fillets

Prep Time: 15 minutes | Cook Time: 12 minutes | Serves: 4

1 pound chicken fillets, boneless, skinless
2 eggs, whisked
1 teaspoon dried basil
½ teaspoon dried rosemary
½ teaspoon dried oregano
½ teaspoon red pepper flakes, crushed
½ cup seasoned breadcrumbs
2 ounces Kalamata olives, pitted and sliced

1. Pat the chicken dry with paper towels. In a shallow bowl, thoroughly combine the eggs and spices. Place the breadcrumbs in a separate shallow bowl. 2. Dip the chicken fillets into the egg mixture, and then roll the chicken fillets over the breadcrumbs. 3. Place the Crisper Tray in the bottom position. Add the chicken to it and close the lid. 4. Move SmartSwitch to AIR FRY/STOVETOP, set the cooking temperature to 380 degrees F and the cooking time to 12 minutes. 5. Turn the chicken over halfway through. Serve with Kalamata olives and enjoy!
Per Serving: Calories 269; Fat 10.08g; Sodium 1589mg; Carbs 11.69g; Fiber 3g; Sugar 2.55g; Protein 28.62g

Spinach Stuffed Chicken

Prep Time: 25 minutes | Cook Time: 20 minutes | Serves: 4

1 pound chicken breasts, skinless, boneless and cut into pieces
2 tablespoons olives, chopped
1 garlic clove, minced
2 cups spinach, torn into pieces
2 ounces feta cheese
Sea salt and ground black pepper, to taste
2 tablespoons olive oil

1. Flatten the chicken breasts with a mallet. Stuff each piece of chicken with olives, garlic, spinach, and cheese. Roll them up and secure with toothpicks. 2. Sprinkle the chicken with the salt, black pepper, and olive oil. 3. Place the Crisper Tray in the bottom position. Add the chicken to it and close the lid. 4. Move SmartSwitch to AIR FRY/STOVETOP, set the cooking temperature to 400 degrees F and the cooking time to 20 minutes. 5. Turn the chicken over halfway through. Serve and enjoy.
Per Serving: Calories 306; Fat 20.79g; Sodium 245mg; Carbs 2.7g; Fiber 0.6g; Sugar 1.22g; Protein 26.4g

Savory Chicken Drumsticks

Prep Time: 25 minutes | Cook Time: 22 minutes | Serves: 3

3 chicken drumsticks
2 tablespoons sesame oil
Kosher salt and ground black pepper, to taste
1 tablespoon soy sauce
1 teaspoon Five-spice powder

1. Pat the chicken drumsticks dry with paper towels. Toss the chicken drumsticks with the remaining ingredients. 2. Place the Crisper Tray in the bottom position. Add the chicken to it and close the lid. Move SmartSwitch to AIR FRY/STOVETOP, set the cooking temperature to 370 degrees F and the cooking time to 22 minutes. 3. Turn the chicken over halfway through. Serve and enjoy.
Per Serving: Calories 314; Fat 22.03g; Sodium 220mg; Carbs 3.52g; Fiber 0.5g; Sugar 1.84g; Protein 24.27g

Sriracha Turkey Breasts

Prep Time: 65 minutes | Cook Time: 20 minutes | Serves: 5

2 pounds turkey breasts, rib bones trimmed
4 tablespoons butter, melted
1 teaspoon Sriracha sauce
1 tablespoon fresh cilantro, chopped
1 tablespoon fresh parsley, chopped
1 tablespoon fresh thyme, chopped
Kosher salt and freshly ground black pepper, to taste

1. Pat the turkey breasts dry with paper towels. Toss the turkey breasts with the remaining ingredients. 2. Place the Crisper Tray in the bottom position. Add the turkey to it and close the lid. Move SmartSwitch to AIR FRY/STOVETOP, set the cooking temperature to 350 degrees F and the cooking time to 60 minutes. 3. Turn the turkey over every 20 minutes. 4. Serve and enjoy.
Per Serving: Calories 369; Fat 21.98g; Sodium 188mg; Carbs 0.55g; Fiber 0.2g; Sugar 0.06g; Protein 39.93g

Hot Chicken Drumsticks

Prep Time: 25 minutes | Cook Time: 20 minutes | Serves: 4

½ cup all-purpose flour
1 tablespoon Ranch seasoning mix
1 pound chicken drumsticks
1 tablespoon hot sauce
Sea salt and ground black pepper, to taste

1. Pat the chicken drumsticks dry with paper towels. Toss the chicken drumsticks with the remaining ingredients. 2. Place the Crisper Tray in the bottom position. Add the chicken to it and close the lid. Move SmartSwitch to AIR FRY/STOVETOP, set the cooking temperature to 370 degrees F and the cooking time to 20 minutes. 3. Turn the chicken over halfway through. 4. Serve and enjoy.

Per Serving: Calories 249; Fat 10.61g; Sodium 307mg; Carbs 13.97g; Fiber 0.9g; Sugar 0.46g; Protein 22.34g

Butter Duck Roast

Prep Time: 45 minutes | Cook Time: 30 minutes | Serves: 5

2 pounds duck breasts
1 tablespoon butter, melted
2 tablespoons pomegranate molasses
2 tablespoons miso paste
1 teaspoon garlic, minced
1 teaspoon ginger, peeled and minced
1 teaspoon Five-spice powder

1. Pat the duck breasts dry with paper towels. Toss the duck breast with the remaining ingredients. 2. Place the Crisper Tray in the bottom position. Add the duck breasts to it and close the lid. Move SmartSwitch to AIR FRY/STOVETOP, set the cooking temperature to 400 degrees F and the cooking time to 15 minutes. 3. Turn the meat over halfway through. When the cooking time is up, turn the heat to 350 degrees F and continue to cook the meat for about 15 minutes or until cooked through. 4. Let it rest for 10 minutes before carving and serving.

Per Serving: Calories 353; Fat 11.75g; Sodium 379mg; Carbs 25.53g; Fiber 5g; Sugar 15.89g; Protein 38.81g

Sicilian Chicken Pieces

Prep Time: 20 minutes | Cook Time: 12 minutes | Serves: 4

1½ pounds chicken fillets
2 tablespoons olive oil
1 teaspoon smoked paprika
1 teaspoon Italian seasoning mix
Sea salt and ground black pepper, to taste
½ cup Pecorino Romano cheese, grated

1. Pat the chicken fillets dry with paper towels. Toss the chicken fillets with the olive oil and spices. 2. Place the Crisper Tray in the bottom position. Add the chicken to it and close the lid. 3. Move SmartSwitch to AIR FRY/STOVETOP, set the cooking temperature to 380 degrees F and the cooking time to 12 minutes. 4. Turn the chicken over halfway through. Top the chicken fillets with grated cheese and serve warm.

Per Serving: Calories 609; Fat 29.54g; Sodium 1350mg; Carbs 57.86g; Fiber 3.3g; Sugar 5.39g; Protein 27.44g

Delicious Chicken Nuggets

Prep Time: 15 minutes | Cook Time: 12 minutes | Serves: 4

1 egg, whisked
¼ cup all-purpose flour
1 cup seasoned breadcrumbs
1 tablespoon olive oil
Sea salt and ground black pepper, to taste
1½ pounds chicken breasts, cut into small pieces

1. Mix the egg and flour in a shallow bowl. In a separate bowl, whisk the breadcrumbs, olive oil, salt, and black pepper. 2. Dip the chicken breasts into the egg mixture, and then roll the chicken breasts over the breadcrumb mixture. Place the Crisper Tray in the bottom position. 3. Add the chicken to it and close the lid. Move SmartSwitch to AIR FRY/STOVETOP, set the cooking temperature to 380 degrees F and the cooking time to 12 minutes. 4. Turn the chicken over halfway through. Serve and enjoy.

Per Serving: Calories 498; Fat 21.62; Sodium 2597mg; Carbs 27.13g; Fiber 4.9g; Sugar 4.46g; Protein 40.28g

Turkey Taquitos Ever

Prep Time: 30 minutes | Cook Time: 25 minutes | Serves: 6

1 pound turkey breasts, boneless and skinless
Kosher salt and freshly ground black pepper, to taste
1 clove garlic, minced
1 habanero pepper, minced
4 ounces Mexican cheese blend, shredded
6 small corn tortillas
½ cup salsa

1. Pat the turkey breasts dry with kitchen towels. Toss the turkey breasts with the salt and black pepper. 2. Place the Crisper Tray in the bottom position. Add the turkey breats to it and close the lid. Move SmartSwitch to AIR FRY/STOVETOP, set the cooking temperature to 380 degrees F and the cooking time to 18 minutes. 3. Turn the meat over halfway through. Place the shredded chicken, garlic, habanero pepper, and cheese on one end of each tortilla. 4. Roll them up tightly and transfer them to the tray. Bake the taquitos at 360 degrees F for 6 minutes more. 5. Serve your taquitos with salsa and enjoy!
Per Serving: Calories 250; Fat 11.45g; Sodium 273mg; Carbs 13.62g; Fiber 2.1g; Sugar 1.69g; Protein 22.92g

Chicken Breasts with Tomatoes

Prep Time: 5 minutes | Cook Time: 25 minutes | Serves: 4

4 chicken breasts, skinless, boneless and halved
2 zucchinis, sliced
4 tomatoes, cut into wedges
2 yellow bell peppers, cut into wedges
2 tablespoons olive oil
1 teaspoon Italian seasoning

1. Mix all of the ingredients and then transfer to the Crisper Tray. 2. Move SmartSwitch to AIR FRY/STOVETOP, set the cooking temperature to 380 degrees F and the cooking time to 20 minutes. 3. Divide everything between plates and serve.
Per Serving: Calories 241; Fat: 17.52g; Sodium: 539mg; Carbs: 9.84g; Fiber: 1.9g; Sugar: 3.56g; Protein: 10.72g calories 280, fat 12, fiber 4, carbs 6, protein 14

Onion Chicken Patties

Prep Time: 20 minutes | Cook Time: 17 minutes | Serves: 4

1 pound chicken, ground
1 tablespoon olive oil
1 small onion, chopped
1 teaspoon garlic, minced
1 tablespoon chili sauce
Kosher salt and ground black pepper, to taste

1. Mix all ingredients until everything is well combined. Form the mixture into four patties. 2. Place the Crisper Tray in the bottom position. Add the patties to it and close the lid. 3. Move SmartSwitch to AIR FRY/STOVETOP, set the cooking temperature to 380 degrees F and the cooking time to 17 minutes. 4. Flip the food halfway through. Serve and enjoy.
Per Serving: Calories 173; Fat 6.49g; Sodium 144mg; Carbs3.78g; Fiber 0.7g; Sugar 1.77g; Protein 23.62g

Okra Chicken Thighs

Prep Time: 10 minutes | Cook Time: 30 minutes | Serves: 4

4 chicken thighs, bone-in and skinless
A pinch of salt and black pepper
1 cup okra
½ cup butter, melted
Zest of 1 lemon, grated
4 garlic cloves, minced
1 tablespoon thyme, chopped
1 tablespoon parsley, chopped

1. Heat up a pan with half of the butter over medium heat, add the chicken thighs and brown them for 2-3 minutes on each side. 2. Add the rest of the butter, the okra and all the remaining ingredients, toss, put the pan on the Crisper Tray. Roast the food at 370 degrees F for 20 minutes. 3. Divide the dish between plates and serve.
Per Serving: Calories 241; Fat: 17.52g; Sodium: 539mg; Carbs: 9.84g; Fiber: 1.9g; Sugar: 3.56g; Protein: 10.72g calories 270, fat 12, fiber 4, carbs 6, protein 14

Butter Chicken Wings

Prep Time: 10 minutes | Cook Time: 30 minutes | Serves: 4

2 pounds chicken wings
Salt and black pepper to the taste
3 garlic cloves, minced
3 tablespoons butter, melted
½ cup heavy cream
½ teaspoon basil, dried
½ teaspoon oregano, dried
¼ cup Parmesan, grated

1. In a baking dish that fits your air fryer, mix the chicken wings with all the ingredients except the Parmesan and toss. Put the dish on the Crisper Tray and Bake the food at 380 degrees F for 30 minutes. 2. Sprinkle the cheese on top, leave the mix aside for 10 minutes, divide between plates and serve.

Per Serving: Calories 241; Fat: 17.52g; Sodium: 539mg; Carbs: 9.84g; Fiber: 1.9g; Sugar: 3.56g; Protein: 10.72g calories 270, fat 12, fiber 3, carbs 6, protein 17

Coconut Chicken Breasts

Prep Time: 10 minutes | Cook Time: 20 minutes | Serves: 4

4 chicken breasts, skinless, boneless and halved
4 tablespoons coconut aminos
1 teaspoon olive oil
2 tablespoons stevia
Salt and black pepper to the taste
¼ cup chicken stock
1 tablespoon ginger, grated

1. In a pan that fits the air fryer, combine the chicken with the ginger and all the ingredients in a suitable baking pan. 2. Put the pan on the Crisper Tray and Roast the food at 380 degrees F for 20 minutes, flip the food halfway. 3. Divide the dish between plates and serve with a side salad.

Per Serving: Calories 241; Fat: 17.52g; Sodium: 539mg; Carbs: 9.84g; Fiber: 1.9g; Sugar: 3.56g; Protein: 10.72g calories 256, fat 12, fiber 4, carbs 6, protein 14

Tomato Chicken Breasts Mix

Prep Time: 10 minutes | Cook Time: 20 minutes | Serves: 4

1 pound chicken breast, skinless, boneless
1 tablespoon keto tomato sauce
1 teaspoon avocado oil
½ teaspoon garlic powder

1. In the small bowl mix up tomato sauce, avocado oil, and garlic powder. Then brush the chicken breast with the tomato sauce mixture well. 2. Preheat the air fryer to 385F. Place the chicken breast in the air fryer and cook it for 15 minutes. Then flip it on another side and cook for 3 minutes more. 3. Slice the cooked chicken breast into servings.

Per Serving: Calories 241; Fat: 17.52g; Sodium: 539mg; Carbs: 9.84g; Fiber: 1.9g; Sugar: 3.56g; Protein: 10.72g calories 139, fat 3, fiber 0.2, carbs 2, protein 24.2

Chicken Thighs with Asparagus & Zucchini

Prep Time: 15 minutes | Cook Time: 25 minutes | Serves: 4

1 pound chicken thighs, boneless and skinless
Juice of 1 lemon
2 tablespoons olive oil
3 garlic cloves, minced
1 teaspoon oregano, dried
½ pound asparagus, trimmed and halved
A pinch of salt and black pepper
1 zucchini, halved lengthwise and sliced into half-moons

1. In a bowl, mix the chicken with all the ingredients except the asparagus and the zucchinis, toss and leave aside for 15 minutes. 2. Add the zucchinis and the asparagus, toss, put everything into a pan. Transfer the pan to the Crisper Tray. Roast the food at 380 degrees F for 25 minutes. 3. Serve warm.

Per Serving: Calories 241; Fat: 17.52g; Sodium: 539mg; Carbs: 9.84g; Fiber: 1.9g; Sugar: 3.56g; Protein: 10.72g calories 280, fat 11, fiber 4, carbs 6, protein 17

Coconut Chicken Fillets

Prep Time: 15 minutes | Cook Time: 15 minutes | Serves: 4

12 oz. chicken fillet (3 oz. each fillet)
4 teaspoons coconut flakes
1 egg white, whisked
1 teaspoon salt
½ teaspoon ground black pepper
Cooking spray

1. Beat the chicken fillets with the kitchen hammer and sprinkle with salt and ground black pepper. Then dip every chicke chop in the whisked egg white and coat in the coconut flakes. 2. Preheat the air fryer to 360F. Put the chicken chops in the ai fryer and spray with cooking spray. Cook the chicken chop for 7 minutes. 3. Then flip them on another side and cook for 5 minutes. The cooked chicken chops should have a golden brown color.

Per Serving: Calories 241; Fat: 17.52g; Sodium: 539mg; Carbs: 9.84g; Fiber: 1.9g; Sugar: 3.56g; Protein: 10.72g calorie 172, fat 6.9, fiber 0.2, carbs 0.5, protein 25.6

Chicken Olives Mix

Prep Time: 10 minutes | Cook Time: 30 minutes | Serves: 4

8 chicken thighs, boneless and skinless
A pinch of salt and black pepper
2 tablespoons olive oil
1 teaspoon oregano, dried
½ teaspoon garlic powder
1 cup pepperoncini, drained and sliced
½ cup black olives, pitted and sliced
½ cup kalamata olives, pitted and sliced
¼ cup Parmesan, grated

1. Heat up a pan that fits the air fryer with the oil over medium-high heat, add the chicken and brown for 2 minutes on eac side. Add salt, pepper, and all the other ingredients except the parmesan and toss. 2. Put the pan on the Crisper Tray and sprinkle th Parmesan on top. Roast the food at 370 degrees F for 25 minutes. 3. Divide the chicken mix between plates and serve.

Per Serving: Calories 241; Fat: 17.52g; Sodium: 539mg; Carbs: 9.84g; Fiber: 1.9g; Sugar: 3.56g; Protein: 10.72g calorie 270, fat 14, fiber 4, carbs 6, protein 18

Basil Pesto Chicken Wings

Prep Time: 10 minutes | Cook Time: 25 minutes | Serves: 4

1 cup basil pesto
2 tablespoons olive oil
A pinch of salt and black pepper
1½ pounds chicken wings

1. In a bowl, mix the chicken wings with all the ingredients and toss well. Transfer the food to the Crisper Tray. 2. Mov SmartSwitch to AIR FRY/STOVETOP, set the cooking temperature to 380 degrees F and the cooking time to 25 minutes. 3 Divide the chicken wings between plates and serve.

Per Serving: Calories 241; Fat: 17.52g; Sodium: 539mg; Carbs: 9.84g; Fiber: 1.9g; Sugar: 3.56g; Protein: 10.72g calorie 244, fat 11, fiber 4, carbs 6, protein 17

Spiced Chicken Breasts

Prep Time: 5 minutes | Cook Time: 20 minutes | Serves: 4

4 chicken breasts, skinless and boneless
1 teaspoon chili powder
A pinch of salt and black pepper
A drizzle of olive oil
1 teaspoon smoked paprika
1 teaspoon garlic powder
1 tablespoon parsley, chopped

1. Season chicken with salt and pepper, and rub it with the oil and all the other ingredients except the parsley. Transfer the food to th Crisper Tray. 2. Move SmartSwitch to AIR FRY/STOVETOP, set the cooking temperature to 350 degrees F and the cooking time 20 minutes. 3. Flip the food halfway through cooking. Divide between plates, sprinkle the parsley on top and serve.

Per Serving: Calories 241; Fat: 17.52g; Sodium: 539mg; Carbs: 9.84g; Fiber: 1.9g; Sugar: 3.56g; Protein: 10.72g calori 222, fat 11, fiber 4, carbs 6, protein 12

Homemade Hens with Onions

Prep Time: 20 minutes | Cook Time: 65 minutes | Serves: 4

14 oz. hen (chicken)
1 teaspoon lemongrass
1 teaspoon ground coriander
1 oz celery stalk, chopped
1 teaspoon dried cilantro
3 spring onions, diced
2 tablespoons avocado oil
2 tablespoons lime juice
½ teaspoon lemon zest, grated
1 teaspoon salt
1 tablespoon apple cider vinegar
1 teaspoon chili powder
½ teaspoon ground black pepper

1. In the mixing bowl mix up lemongrass, ground coriander, dried cilantro, lime juice, lemon zest, salt, apple cider vinegar, and ground black pepper. Then add spring onions and celery stalk. 2. After this, rub the hen with the spice mixture and leave for 10 minutes to marinate. Transfer the food to the Crisper Tray. 3. Move SmartSwitch to AIR FRY/STOVETOP, set the cooking temperature to 375 degrees F and the cooking time to 65 minutes. 4. Flip the food after 45 minutes of cooking time.

Per Serving: Calories 241; Fat: 17.52g; Sodium: 539mg; Carbs: 9.84g; Fiber: 1.9g; Sugar: 3.56g; Protein: 10.72g calories 177, fat 4.1, fiber 1.41, carbs 4.4, protein 29.3

Provolone Chicken Meatballs

Prep Time: 10 minutes | Cook Time: 12 minutes | Serves: 6

12 oz ground chicken
½ cup coconut flour
2 egg whites, whisked
1 teaspoon ground black pepper
1 egg yolk
1 teaspoon salt
4 oz Provolone cheese, grated
1 teaspoon ground oregano
½ teaspoon chili powder
1 tablespoon avocado oil

1. In the mixing bowl mix up ground chicken, ground black pepper, egg yolk, salt, Provolone cheese, ground oregano, and chili powder. Stir the mixture until homogenous and make the small meatballs. 2. Dip the meatballs in the whisked egg whites and coat in the coconut flour. Transfer the food to the Crisper Tray. 3. Move SmartSwitch to AIR FRY/STOVETOP, set the cooking temperature to 370 degrees F and the cooking time to 6 minutes.

Per Serving: Calories 241; Fat: 17.52g; Sodium: 539mg; Carbs: 9.84g; Fiber: 1.9g; Sugar: 3.56g; Protein: 10.72g calories 234, fat 11.7, fiber 3.7, carbs 6.6, protein 24.3

Ghee Chicken Legs

Prep Time: 15 minutes | Cook Time: 30 minutes | Serves: 4

12 oz chicken legs
1 teaspoon nutritional yeast
1 teaspoon chili flakes
½ teaspoon ground cumin
½ teaspoon garlic powder
1 teaspoon ground turmeric
½ teaspoon ground paprika
1 teaspoon Splenda
¼ cup coconut flour
1 tablespoon ghee, melted

1. In the mixing bowl mix up nutritional yeast, chili flakes, ground cumin, garlic powder, ground turmeric, ground paprika, Splenda, and coconut flour. 2. Then brush every chicken leg with ghee and coat well in the coconut flour mixture. Preheat the air fryer to 380F. Place the chicken legs in the air fryer in one layer. 3. Cook them for 15 minutes. Then flip the chicken legs on another side and cook them for 15 minutes more.

Per Serving: Calories 241; Fat: 17.52g; Sodium: 539mg; Carbs: 9.84g; Fiber: 1.9g; Sugar: 3.56g; Protein: 10.72g calories 238, fat 10.9, fiber 3.5, carbs 6.8, protein 26.7

Chicken with Sun-dried Tomatoes

Prep Time: 5 minutes | Cook Time: 25 minutes | Serves: 4

4 chicken thighs, skinless, boneless
1 tablespoon olive oil
A pinch of salt and black pepper
1 tablespoon thyme, chopped
1 cup chicken stock
3 garlic cloves, minced
½ cup coconut cream
1 cup sun-dried tomatoes, chopped
4 tablespoons parmesan, grated

1. Heat up a pan with the oil over medium-high heat, add the chicken, salt, pepper and the garlic, and brown for 2-3 minutes on each side. 2. Add the rest of the ingredients except the Parmesan, toss, put the pan on the Crisper Tray and Roast the food at 370 degrees F for 20 minutes. 3. Sprinkle the Parmesan on top, leave the mix sit for 5 minutes, divide everything between plates and serve.
Per Serving: Calories 241; Fat: 17.52g; Sodium: 539mg; Carbs: 9.84g; Fiber: 1.9g; Sugar: 3.56g; Protein: 10.72g calories 275, fat 12, fiber 4, carbs 6, protein 17

Cauliflower Stuffed Chicken Breasts

Prep Time: 20 minutes | Cook Time: 25 minutes | Serves: 5

1½-pound chicken breast, skinless, boneless
½ cup cauliflower, shredded
1 jalapeno pepper, chopped
1 teaspoon ground nutmeg
1 teaspoon salt
¼ cup Cheddar cheese, shredded
½ teaspoon cayenne pepper
1 tablespoon cream cheese
1 tablespoon sesame oil
½ teaspoon dried thyme

1. Make the horizontal cut in the chicken breast. In the mixing bowl mix up shredded cauliflower, chopped jalapeno pepper, ground nutmeg, salt, and cayenne pepper. 2. Fill the chicken cut with the shredded cauliflower and secure the cut with toothpicks. Then rub the chicken breast with cream cheese, dried thyme, and sesame oil. 3. Transfer the chicken breasts to the Crisper Tray. Move SmartSwitch to AIR FRY/STOVETOP, set the cooking temperature to 380 degrees F and the cooking time to 20 minutes. 4. Sprinkle the dish with Cheddar cheese and cook for 5 minutes more.
Per Serving: Calories 241; Fat: 17.52g; Sodium: 539mg; Carbs: 9.84g; Fiber: 1.9g; Sugar: 3.56g; Protein: 10.72g calories 266, fat 9.6, fiber 0.5, carbs 1.2, protein 41.3

Chapter 4 Beef, Pork, and Lamb Recipes

German Schnitzel

Prep Time: 5 minutes | Cook Time: 12 minutes | Serves: 4

4 thin beef schnitzel
1 tbsp. sesame seeds
2 tbsp. paprika
3 tbsp. olive oil
4 tbsp. flour
2 eggs, beaten
1 cup friendly bread crumbs
Pepper and salt to taste

1. Sprinkle the pepper and salt on the schnitzel. 2. In a shallow dish, combine the paprika, flour, and salt. In a second shallow dish, mix the bread crumbs with the sesame seeds. 3. Place the beaten eggs in a bowl. Coat the schnitzel in the flour mixture. Dip it into the egg before rolling it in the bread crumbs. 4. Place the Crisper Tray in the bottom position. Add the coated schnitzel to it and close the lid. Move SmartSwitch to AIR FRY/STOVETOP, set the cooking temperature to 400 degrees F and the cooking time to 12 minutes. 5. Serve and enjoy.

Per Serving: Calories 348; Fat 29.13g; Sodium 77mg; Carbs 8.96g; Fiber 1.8g; Sugar 0.5g; Protein 13.54g

Rib Eye Steak

Prep Time: 15 minutes | Cook Time: 14 minutes | Serves: 4

2 lb. rib eye steak
1 tbsp. olive oil
1 tbsp. steak rub

1. Massage the olive oil and steak rub into both sides of the steak. 2. Place the Crisper Tray in the bottom position. Add the steak to it and close the lid. Move SmartSwitch to AIR FRY/STOVETOP, set the cooking temperature to 400 degrees F and the cooking time to 14 minutes. 3. Flip the food halfway through. Serve hot.

Per Serving: Calories 624; Fat 50.92g; Sodium 199mg; Carbs 0.94g; Fiber 0.1g; Sugar 0.42g; Protein 40.7g

Savory Beef Roast

Prep Time: 10 minutes | Cook Time: 55 minutes | Serves: 6

2 lb. beef
1 tbsp. olive oil
1 tsp. dried rosemary
1 tsp. dried thyme
½ tsp. black pepper
½ tsp. oregano
½ tsp. garlic powder
1 tsp. salt
1 tsp. onion powder

1. In a small bowl, mix together all of the spices. Coat the beef with a brushing of olive oil. 2. Massage the spice mixture into the beef. Place the Crisper Tray in the bottom position. 3. Add the food to it and close the lid. Move SmartSwitch to AIR FRY/STOVETOP, set the cooking temperature to 330 degrees F and the cooking time to 30 minutes. 4. Turn the food over halfway through. Serve hot.

Per Serving: Calories 224; Fat 10.91g; Sodium 518mg; Carbs 0.78g; Fiber 0.2g; Sugar 0.04g; Protein 31.16g

Easy Beef Steak

Prep Time: 10 minutes | Cook Time: 6 minutes | Serves: 1

1 steak, 1-inch thick
1 tbsp. olive oil
Black pepper to taste
Sea salt to taste

1. Place the baking tray inside the Air Fryer and pre-heat for about 5 minutes at 390°F. 2. Brush or spray both sides of the steak with the oil. Season both sides with salt and pepper. Place the Crisper Tray in the bottom position. 3. Add the steak to it and close the lid. Move SmartSwitch to AIR FRY/STOVETOP, set the cooking temperature to 350 degrees F and the cooking time to 6 minutes. 4. Flip the steak halfway through. Let the dish rest for 3 minutes before serving.

Per Serving: Calories 614; Fat 46.23g; Sodium 263mg; Carbs 0.06g; Fiber 0g; Sugar 0g; Protein 46.39g

Sausage & Beef Meatloaf

Prep Time: 5 minutes | Cook Time: 25 minutes | Serves: 4

¾ lb. ground chuck
¼ lb. ground pork sausage
1 cup shallots, finely chopped
2 eggs, well beaten
3 tbsp. plain milk
1 tbsp. oyster sauce
1 tsp. porcini mushrooms
½ tsp. cumin powder
1 tsp. garlic paste
1 tbsp. fresh parsley
Seasoned salt and crushed red pepper flakes to taste
1 cup crushed saltines

1. Mix together all of the ingredients in a large bowl. Place the Crisper Tray in the bottom position. 2. Add the food to it and close the lid. Move SmartSwitch to AIR FRY/STOVETOP, set the cooking temperature to 360 degrees F and the cooking time to 25 minutes. 3. Serve hot.

Per Serving: Calories 249; Fat 14.03g; Sodium 417mg; Carbs 11.21g; Fiber 0.6g; Sugar 1.48g; Protein 19.3g

Beef Stuffed Bell Pepper

Prep Time: 10 minutes | Cook Time: 15-20 minutes | Serves: 4

4 bell peppers, cut top of bell pepper
16 oz. ground beef
⅔ cup cheese, shredded
½ cup rice, cooked
1 tsp. basil, dried
½ tsp. chili powder
1 tsp. black pepper
1 tsp. garlic salt
2 tsp. Worcestershire sauce
8 oz. tomato sauce
2 garlic cloves, minced
1 small onion, chopped

1. Grease a frying pan with cooking spray and fry the onion and garlic in it over a medium heat. Add the beef, basil, chili powder, black pepper, and garlic salt, and allow them to cook until the beef is nicely browned. 2. Turn off the heat. Add in half of the cheese, the rice, Worcestershire sauce, and tomato sauce and stir to combine. 3. Spoon equal amounts of the beef mixture into the four bell peppers, filling them entirely. Place the Crisper Tray in the elevated position. 4. Add the food to it and close the lid. Move SmartSwitch to RAPID COOKER, and then use the center front arrows to select Steam & Crisp. Set the cooking temperature to 400 degrees F and the cooking time to 13 minutes. 5. Add the remaining cheese on top of each bell pepper with remaining cheese after 11 minutes of cooking time. 6. When done, the cheese should be melted and the bell peppers should be piping hot. Serve hot.

Per Serving: Calories 548; Fat 44.13g; Sodium 264mg; Carbs 17g; Fiber 4.8g; Sugar 3.62g; Protein 25.58g

Spiced Beef Burgers

Prep Time: 8 minutes | Cook Time: 12 minutes | Serves: 4

¾ lb. lean ground beef
1 tbsp. soy sauce
1 tsp. Dijon mustard
Few dashes of liquid smoke
1 tsp. shallot powder
1 clove garlic, minced
½ tsp. cumin powder
¼ cup scallions, minced
⅓ tsp. sea salt flakes
⅓ tsp. freshly cracked mixed peppercorns
1 tsp. celery seeds
1 tsp. parsley flakes

1. Mix together all of the ingredients in a bowl using your hands, combining everything well. 2. Take four equal amounts of the mixture and mold each one into a patty. 3. Use the back of a spoon to create a shallow dip in the center of each patty. This will prevent them from puffing up during the cooking process. 4. Lightly coat all sides of the patties with cooking spray. Place the Crisper Tray in the bottom position. 5. Add the patties to it and close the lid. Move SmartSwitch to AIR FRY/STOVETOP, set the cooking temperature to 360 degrees F and the cooking time to 12 minutes. 6. The patties are ready once they have reached 160°F. Serve them on top of butter rolls with any sauces and toppings you desire.

Per Serving: Calories 203; Fat 10.62g; Sodium 326mg; Carbs 2.19g; Fiber 0.4g; Sugar 0.98g; Protein 23.3g

Cheese Beef Patties

Prep Time: 5 minutes | Cook Time: 11 minutes | Serves: 6

1 lb. ground beef
6 cheddar cheese slices
Pepper and salt to taste

1. Sprinkle the salt and pepper on the ground beef. Shape six equal portions of the ground beef into patties. 2. Place the Crispe Tray in the bottom position. Add the patties to it and close the lid. Move SmartSwitch to AIR FRY/STOVETOP, set th cooking temperature to 350 degrees F and the cooking time to 10 minutes. 3. Top the patties with the cheese slices and air fr for one more minute. 4. Serve the patties on top of dinner rolls.
Per Serving: Calories 276; Fat 17.86g; Sodium 226mg; Carbs 0.38g; Fiber 0g; Sugar 0.08g; Protein 26.86g

Beef Steak Rolls

Prep Time: 20 minutes | Cook Time: 10 minutes | Serves: 2

2 lb. beef flank steak
3 tsp. pesto
1 tsp. black pepper
6 slices of provolone cheese
3 oz. roasted red bell peppers
¾ cup baby spinach
1 tsp. sea salt

1. Spoon equal amounts of the pesto onto each flank steak and spread it across evenly. 2. Place the cheese, roasted red pepper and spinach on top of the meat, about three-quarters of the way down. 3. Roll the steak up, holding it in place with toothpicks Sprinkle on the sea salt and pepper. 4. Place the Crisper Tray in the bottom position. Add the food to it and close the lid. Mov SmartSwitch to AIR FRY/STOVETOP, set the cooking temperature to 400 degrees F and the cooking time to 10 minutes. 5 Turn the rolls over halfway through. Allow the beef to rest for 10 minutes before slicing up and serving.
Per Serving: Calories 1015; Fat 53.55g; Sodium 2386mg; Carbs 6.34g; Fiber 1.3g; Sugar 2.52g; Protein 121.04g

Beef Schnitzel with Lemon Wedges

Prep Time: 15 minutes | Cook Time: 15 minutes | Serves: 1

1 egg
1 thin beef schnitzel
3 tbsp. friendly bread crumbs
2 tbsp. olive oil
1 parsley, roughly chopped
½ lemon, cut in wedges

1. In a bowl combine the bread crumbs and olive oil to form a loose, crumbly mixture. 2. Beat the egg with a whisk. Coa the schnitzel first in the egg and then in the bread crumbs, ensuring to cover it fully. 3. Place the Crisper Tray in the botton position. Add the schinitzel to it and close the lid. Move SmartSwitch to AIR FRY/STOVETOP, set the cooking temperature t 360 degrees F and the cooking time to 14 minutes. 4. Garnish the schnitzel with the lemon wedges and parsley before serving.
Per Serving: Calories 582; Fat 47.91g; Sodium 284mg; Carbs 20.38g; Fiber 3g; Sugar 2.54g; Protein 19.34g

Onion Beef Meatballs

Prep Time: 5 minutes | Cook Time: 15 minutes | Serves: 4

1 egg
½ lb. beef minced
½ cup friendly breadcrumbs
1 tbsp. parsley, chopped
2 tbsp. raisins
1 cup onion, chopped and fried
½ tbsp. pepper
½ tsp. salt

1. Place all of the ingredients in a bowl and combine well. Shape equal amounts of the mixture into small balls. Place th Crisper Tray in the bottom position. 2. Add the food to it and close the lid. Move SmartSwitch to AIR FRY/STOVETOP, se the cooking temperature to 350 degrees F and the cooking time to 15 minutes. 3. Serve the dish with the sauce you like.
Per Serving: Calories 142; Fat 5.93g; Sodium 380mg; Carbs 9.01g; Fiber 2.2g; Sugar 2.79g; Protein 14.94g

Vegetables & Beef Rolls

Prep Time: 25 minutes | Cook Time: 10 minutes | Serves: 20

⅓ cup noodles
1 cup beef minced
2 tbsp. cold water
1 packet spring roll sheets
1 tsp. soy sauce
1 cup fresh mix vegetables
3 garlic cloves, minced
1 small onion, diced
1 tbsp. sesame oil

1. Cook the noodle in hot water to soften them up, drain them and snip them to make them shorter. 2. In a frying pan over medium heat, cook the minced beef, soy sauce, mixed vegetables, garlic, and onion in a little oil until the beef minced is cooked through. 3. Take the pan off the heat and throw in the noodles. Mix well to incorporate everything. 4. Unroll a spring roll sheet and lay it flat. Scatter the filling diagonally across it and roll it up, brushing the edges lightly with water to act as an adhesive. Repeat until you have used up all of the sheets and the filling. 5. Coat each spring roll with a light brushing of oil. Place the Crisper Tray in the bottom position. 6. Add the food to it and close the lid. Move SmartSwitch to AIR FRY/STOVETOP, set the cooking temperature to 350 degrees F and the cooking time to 8 minutes. 7. Serve hot.
Per Serving: Calories 39; Fat 1.48g; Sodium 32mg; Carbs 3.59g; Fiber 0.5g; Sugar 0.62g; Protein 3g

Cheese Beef Schnitzel

Prep Time: 5 minutes | Cook Time: 15 minutes | Serves: 1

1 thin beef schnitzel
1 egg, beaten
½ cup friendly bread crumbs
2 tbsp. olive oil
3 tbsp. pasta sauce
¼ cup parmesan cheese, grated
Pepper and salt to taste

1. In a shallow dish, combine the bread crumbs, olive oil, pepper, and salt. In another shallow dish, put the beaten egg. 2. Cover the schnitzel in the egg before press it into the breadcrumb mixture. 3. Place the Crisper Tray in the elevated position. Add the food to it and close the lid. Move SmartSwitch to RAPID COOKER, and then use the center front arrows to select Steam & Crisp. Set the cooking temperature to 350 degrees F and the cooking time to 20 minutes. 4. Pour the pasta sauce over the schnitzel and top with the grated cheese after 15 minutes of cooking time. Serve hot.
Per Serving: Calories 354; Fat 7.9g; Sodium 704mg; Carbs 6g; Fiber 3.6g; Sugar 6g; Protein 18g

Breakfast Beef Cups

Prep Time: 10 minutes | Cook Time: 25 minutes | Serves: 4

Meatloaves:
1 pound ground beef
¼ cup seasoned breadcrumbs
¼ cup parmesan cheese, grated
1 small onion, minced
2 garlic cloves, pressed
1 egg, beaten
Sea salt and ground black pepper, to taste
Glaze:
4 tablespoons tomato sauce
1 tablespoon brown sugar
1 tablespoon Dijon mustard

1. Thoroughly combine all ingredients for the meatloaves until everything is well combined. Scrape the beef mixture into lightly oiled silicone cups, and then place the cups on the Crisper Tray. 2. Bake the food at 380 degrees F for 20 minutes. Mix the remaining ingredients for the glaze. 3. Then, spread the glaze on top of each muffin; continue to cook them for another 5 minutes. Serve and enjoy.
Per Serving: Calories 241; Fat: 17.52g; Sodium: 539mg; Carbs: 9.84g; Fiber: 1.9g; Sugar: 3.56g; Protein: 10.72g

Beef & Broccoli Florets

Prep Time: 50 minutes | Cook Time: 12 minutes | Serves: 4

1 lb. broccoli, cut into florets
¾ lb. round steak, cut into strips
1 garlic clove, minced
1 tsp. ginger, minced
1 tbsp. olive oil
1 tsp. cornstarch
1 tsp. sugar
1 tsp. soy sauce
⅓ cup sherry wine
2 tsp. sesame oil
⅓ cup oyster sauce

1. In a bowl, combine the sugar, soy sauce, sherry wine, cornstarch, sesame oil, and oyster sauce. 2. Place the steak strips in the bowl, coat each one with the mixture and allow to marinate for 45 minutes. 3. Place the Crisper Tray in the elevated position. Add the broccoli to it and lay the steak on top and then top them with the olive oil, garlic, and ginger. Close the lid. Move SmartSwitch to RAPID COOKER, and then use the center front arrows to select Steam & Crisp. 4. Set the cooking temperature to 350 degrees F and the cooking time to 12 minutes. 5. Serve the dish hot with rice if desired.
Per Serving: Calories 269; Fat 13.06g; Sodium 743mg; Carbs 7.94g; Fiber 3.2g; Sugar 1.52g; Protein 30.22g

Breaded Meatloaf

Prep Time: 10 minutes | Cook Time: 25 minutes | Serves: 4

1 large onion, peeled and diced
2 kg. minced beef
1 tsp. Worcester sauce
3 tbsp. tomato ketchup
1 tbsp. basil
1 tbsp. oregano
1 tbsp. mixed herbs
1 tbsp. friendly bread crumbs
Salt & pepper to taste

1. In a large bowl, combine the mince with the herbs, Worcester sauce, onion and tomato ketchup, incorporating every component well. 2. Pour in the breadcrumbs and give it another stir. Place the Crisper Tray in the bottom position. 3. Add the food to it and close the lid. Move SmartSwitch to AIR FRY/STOVETOP, set the cooking temperature to 350 degrees F and the cooking time to 25 minutes. 4. Serve hot.
Per Serving: Calories 724; Fat 29.1g; Sodium 503mg; Carbs 12.27g; Fiber 1.8g; Sugar 3.84g; Protein 104.71g

Paprika-Seasoned Flank Steak

Prep Time: 10 minutes | Cook Time: 15 minutes | Serves: 5

2 pounds flank steak
2 tablespoons olive oil
1 teaspoon paprika
Sea salt and ground black pepper, to taste

1. Toss the steak with the remaining ingredients. Transfer the food to the Crisper Tray. Move SmartSwitch to AIR FRY/STOVETOP, set the cooking temperature to 400 degrees F and the cooking time to 12 minutes. 2. Flip the steak halfway through. Serve hot.
Per Serving: Calories 241; Fat: 17.52g; Sodium: 539mg; Carbs: 9.84g; Fiber: 1.9g; Sugar: 3.56g; Protein: 10.72g

BBQ Beef Brisket

Prep Time: 10 minutes | Cook Time: 70 minutes | Serves: 4

1½ pounds beef brisket
¼ cup barbecue sauce
2 tablespoons soy sauce

1. Toss the beef with the remaining ingredients. Transfer the food to the Crisper Tray. Move SmartSwitch to AIR FRY/STOVETOP, set the cooking temperature to 390 degrees F and the cooking time to 15 minutes. 2. When the cooking time is up, adjust the cooking temperature to 360 degrees F and then resume cooking the food for 55 minutes more. 3. Serve warm.
Per Serving: Calories 390; Fat: 10g; Sodium: 539mg; Carbs: 9.84g; Fiber: 1.9g; Sugar: 3.56g; Protein: 10.72g

Cream Canadian Bacon

Prep Time: 8 minutes | Cook Time: 10 minutes | Serves: 4

10-ounces Canadian bacon, sliced
1 teaspoon cream
½ teaspoon salt
¼ teaspoon ground black pepper
½ teaspoon ground coriander
½ teaspoon ground thyme

1. In a mixing bowl combine the thyme, coriander, black pepper, and salt. 2. Sprinkle this spice mix on top of the bacon slices on each side. 3. Place the Crisper Tray in the bottom position. Add the food to it and close the lid. Move SmartSwitch to AIR FRY/STOVETOP, set the cooking temperature to 360 degrees F and the cooking time to 10 minutes. 4. Flip the food halfway through. Once the bacon is cooked, remove it from air fryer and sprinkle it with cream and serve immediately!

Per Serving: Calories 82; Fat 2.21g; Sodium 818mg; Carbs 1.25g; Fiber 0.1g; Sugar 0.83g; Protein 14.44g

Tuna & Bacon Slices

Prep Time: 10 minutes | Cook Time: 10 minutes | Serves: 4

6-ounces bacon, sliced
1 teaspoon butter
4-ounces parmesan cheese, shredded
1 teaspoon cream
6-ounces tuna
½ teaspoon ground black pepper
¼ teaspoon turmeric
¼ teaspoon sea salt

1. Place bacon inside of four ramekins. Add a small amount of butter in each ramekin. 2. Mix the sea salt, turmeric, and ground black pepper. Combine chopped tuna with spice mix. 3. Place some tuna mix into each ramekin on top of bacon. Add the cream and shredded cheese on top of tuna mix. 4. Place the Crisper Tray in the elevated position. Add the food to it and close the lid. Move SmartSwitch to RAPID COOKER, and then use the center front arrows to select Steam & Crisp. Set the cooking temperature to 360 degrees F and the cooking time to 10 minutes. 5. When the tuna boards are done cooking, they will have a sweet, crunchy taste with a light brown color to them. 6. Serve hot!

Per Serving: Calories 301; Fat 22.07g; Sodium 1393mg; Carbs 7.34g; Fiber 1.2g; Sugar 0.36g; Protein 21.04g

Chinese-Style Beef Tenderloin

Prep Time: 35 minutes | Cook Time: 20 minutes | Serves: 4

1½ pounds beef tenderloin, sliced
2 tablespoons sesame oil
1 teaspoon Five-spice powder
2 garlic cloves, minced
1 teaspoon fresh ginger, peeled and grated
2 tablespoons soy sauce

1. Toss the beef tenderloin with the remaining ingredients. Transfer the food to the Crisper Tray. 2. Move SmartSwitch to AIR FRY/STOVETOP, set the cooking temperature to 400 degrees F and the cooking time to 20 minutes. 3. Flip the tenderloin halfway through. Serve and enjoy.

Per Serving: Calories 241; Fat: 17.52g; Sodium: 539mg; Carbs: 9.84g; Fiber: 1.9g; Sugar: 3.56g; Protein: 10.72g

Juicy Tomahawk Steaks

Prep Time: 10 minutes | Cook Time: 15 minutes | Serves: 4 15 minutes | Servings 4)

1½ pounds Tomahawk steaks
2 bell peppers, sliced
2 tablespoons butter, melted
2 teaspoons Montreal steak seasoning
2 tablespoons fish sauce
Sea salt and ground black pepper, to taste

1. Toss all ingredients. Transfer the food to the Crisper Tray. Move SmartSwitch to AIR FRY/STOVETOP, set the cooking temperature to 400 degrees F and the cooking time to 14 minutes. 2. Flip the food halfway through. Serve and enjoy.

Per Serving: Calories 241; Fat: 17.52g; Sodium: 539mg; Carbs: 9.84g; Fiber: 1.9g; Sugar: 3.56g; Protein: 10.72g

BBQ Chuck Cheeseburgers

Prep Time: 5 minutes | Cook Time: 15 minutes | Serves: 3

¾ pound ground chuck
1 teaspoon garlic, minced
2 tablespoons BBQ sauce
Sea salt and ground black pepper, to taste
3 slices cheese
3 hamburger buns

1. Mix the ground chuck, garlic, BBQ sauce, salt, and black pepper until everything is well combined. Form the mixture into four patties. Transfer the patties to the Crisper Tray. 2. Move SmartSwitch to AIR FRY/STOVETOP, set the cooking temperature to 380 degrees F and the cooking time to 15 minutes. 3. Flip the patties halfway through cooking. Top each burger with cheese. 4. Serve your burgers on the prepared buns and enjoy.
Per Serving: Calories 241; Fat: 17.52g; Sodium: 539mg; Carbs: 9.84g; Fiber: 1.9g; Sugar: 3.56g; Protein: 10.72g

Butter London Broil

Prep Time: 10 minutes | Cook Time: 30 minutes | Serves: 4

1½ pounds London broil
Kosher salt and ground black pepper, to taste
¼ teaspoon ground bay leaf
3 tablespoons butter, cold
1 tablespoon Dijon mustard
1 teaspoon garlic, pressed
1 tablespoon fresh parsley, chopped

1. Toss the beef with the salt and black pepper. Transfer the food to the Crisper Tray. 2. Move SmartSwitch to AIR FRY/STOVETOP, set the cooking temperature to 400 degrees F and the cooking time to 28 minutes. Flip the beef halfway through cooking. 3. Mix the butter with the remaining ingredients and place it in the refrigerator until well-chilled. Serve warm beef with the chilled garlic butter on the side. 4. Bon appétit!
Per Serving: Calories 241; Fat: 17.52g; Sodium: 539mg; Carbs: 9.84g; Fiber: 1.9g; Sugar: 3.56g; Protein: 10.72g

Typical Mexican Carnitas

Prep Time: 20 minutes | Cook Time: 70 minutes | Serves: 4

1½ pounds beef brisket
2 tablespoons olive oil
Sea salt and ground black pepper, to taste
1 teaspoon chili powder
4 medium-sized flour tortillas

1. Toss the beef brisket with the olive oil, salt, black pepper, and chili powder. Transfer the food to the Crisper Tray. 2. Move SmartSwitch to AIR FRY/STOVETOP, set the cooking temperature to 390 degrees F and the cooking time to 15 minutes. 3. When the cooking time is up, reduce the cooking temperature to 360 degrees F and resume cooking the food for 55 minutes more. 4. Shred the beef with two forks and serve with tortillas and toppings of choice. Bon appétit!
Per Serving: Calories 241; Fat: 17.52g; Sodium: 539mg; Carbs: 9.84g; Fiber: 1.9g; Sugar: 3.56g; Protein: 10.72g

Mexican Meatloaf

Prep Time: 10 minutes | Cook Time: 15 minutes | Serves: 4 30 minutes | Servings 4)

1½ pounds ground chuck
½ onion, chopped
1 teaspoon habanero pepper, minced
¼ cup tortilla chips, crushed
1 teaspoon garlic, minced
Sea salt and ground black pepper, to taste
2 tablespoons olive oil
1 egg, whisked

1. Thoroughly combine all ingredients until everything is well combined. Scrape the beef mixture into a lightly oiled baking pan and place the pan on the Crisper Tray. 2. Roast the food at 390 degrees F for 25 minutes. Serve hot.
Per Serving: Calories 241; Fat: 17.52g; Sodium: 539mg; Carbs: 9.84g; Fiber: 1.9g; Sugar: 3.56g; Protein: 10.72g

Spiced Filet Mignon

Prep Time: 10 minutes | Cook Time: 15 minutes | Serves: 4

1½ pounds filet mignon
Sea salt and ground black pepper, to taste
2 tablespoons olive oil
1 teaspoon dried rosemary
1 teaspoon dried thyme
1 teaspoon dried basil
2 cloves garlic, minced

1. Toss the beef with the remaining ingredients. Transfer the food to the Crisper Tray. 2. Move SmartSwitch to AIR FRY/STOVETOP, set the cooking temperature to 400 degrees F and the cooking time to 15 minutes. 3. Flip the food halfway through cooking. Serve and enjoy.

Per Serving: Calories 241; Fat: 17.52g; Sodium: 539mg; Carbs: 9.84g; Fiber: 1.9g; Sugar: 3.56g; Protein: 10.72g

Rib-eye Steak with Blue Cheese

Prep Time: 10 minutes | Cook Time: 15 minutes | Serves: 4 15 minutes | Servings 4)

1 pound ribeye steak, bone-in
Sea salt and ground black pepper, to taste
2 tablespoons olive oil
½ teaspoon onion powder
1 teaspoon garlic powder
1 cup blue cheese, crumbled

1. Toss the ribeye steak with the salt, black pepper, olive oil, onion powder, and garlic powder. Transfer the food to the Crisper Tray. 2. Move SmartSwitch to AIR FRY/STOVETOP, set the cooking temperature to 400 degrees F and the cooking time to 15 minutes. 3. Flip the steak halfway through cooking. Top the steak with cheese before enjoying.

Per Serving: Calories 241; Fat: 17.52g; Sodium: 539mg; Carbs: 9.84g; Fiber: 1.9g; Sugar: 3.56g; Protein: 10.72g

Rump Roast

Prep Time: 10 minutes | Cook Time: 15 minutes | Serves: 4 55 minutes | Servings 4)

1½ pounds rump roast
Ground black pepper and kosher salt, to taste
1 teaspoon paprika
2 tablespoons olive oil
¼ cup brandy
2 tablespoons cold butter

1. Toss the rump roast with the black pepper, salt, paprika, olive oil, and brandy. Transfer the rump roast to the Crisper Tray. 2. Move SmartSwitch to AIR FRY/STOVETOP, set the cooking temperature to 390 degrees F and the cooking time to 50 minutes. Turn the roast over halfway through. 3. Serve the dish with the cold butter and enjoy!

Per Serving: Calories 241; Fat: 17.52g; Sodium: 539mg; Carbs: 9.84g; Fiber: 1.9g; Sugar: 3.56g; Protein: 10.72g

Flavorful Coulotte Roast

Prep Time: 10 minutes | Cook Time: 55 minutes | Serves: 5

2 pounds Coulotte roast
2 tablespoons olive oil
1 tablespoon fresh parsley, finely chopped
1 tablespoon fresh cilantro, finely chopped
2 garlic cloves, minced
Kosher salt and ground black pepper, to taste

1. Toss the roast beef with the remaining ingredients. Transfer the food to the Crisper Tray. 2. Move SmartSwitch to AIR FRY/STOVETOP, set the cooking temperature to 390 degrees F and the cooking time to 55 minutes. 3. Turn the roast over halfway through the cooking time. Serve and enjoy.

Per Serving: Calories 241; Fat: 17.52g; Sodium: 539mg; Carbs: 9.84g; Fiber: 1.9g; Sugar: 3.56g; Protein: 10.72g

Mushroom Beef Patties

Prep Time: 10 minutes | Cook Time: 15 minutes | Serves: 4 15 minutes | Servings 4)

1 pound ground chuck
2 garlic cloves, minced
1 small onion, chopped
1 cup mushrooms, chopped
1 teaspoon cayenne pepper
Sea salt and ground black pepper, to taste
4 brioche rolls

1. Mix the ground chuck, garlic, onion, mushrooms, cayenne pepper, salt, and black pepper until everything is well combined. Form the mixture into four patties. 2. Transfer the patties to the Crisper Tray. Move SmartSwitch to AIR FRY/STOVETOP, set the cooking temperature to 380 degrees F and the cooking time to 15 minutes. 3. Flip the food halfway through. Serve your patties on the prepared brioche rolls and enjoy!

Per Serving: Calories 241; Fat: 17.52g; Sodium: 539mg; Carbs: 9.84g; Fiber: 1.9g; Sugar: 3.56g; Protein: 10.72g

Simple Steak Salad

Prep Time: 10 minutes | Cook Time: 15 minutes | Serves: 5

2 pounds T-bone steak
1 teaspoon garlic powder
Sea salt and ground black pepper, to taste
2 tablespoons lime juice
¼ cup extra-virgin olive oil
1 bell pepper, seeded and sliced
1 red onion, sliced
1 tomato, diced

1. Toss the steak with the garlic powder, salt, and black pepper. Transfer the food to the Crisper Tray. 2. Move SmartSwitch to AIR FRY/STOVETOP, set the cooking temperature to 400 degrees F and the cooking time to 12 minutes. 3. Flip the steak halfway through. Cut the steak into slices and add in the remaining ingredients. 4. Serve the dish at room temperature or well-chilled.

Per Serving: Calories 241; Fat: 17.52g; Sodium: 539mg; Carbs: 9.84g; Fiber: 1.9g; Sugar: 3.56g; Protein: 10.72g

Beef Sliders

Prep Time: 5 minutes | Cook Time: 15 minutes | Serves: 4

1 pound ground beef
½ teaspoon garlic powder
½ teaspoon onion powder
1 teaspoon paprika
Sea salt and ground black pepper, to taste
8 dinner rolls

1. Mix all ingredients, except for the dinner rolls. Shape the mixture into four patties. Transfer the patties to the Crisper Tray. 2. Move SmartSwitch to AIR FRY/STOVETOP, set the cooking temperature to 380 degrees F and the cooking time to 15 minutes. Flip the patties halfway through. 3. Serve the burgers on the prepared dinner rolls and enjoy!

Per Serving: Calories 241; Fat: 17.52g; Sodium: 539mg; Carbs: 9.84g; Fiber: 1.9g; Sugar: 3.56g; Protein: 10.72g

Tender Filet Mignon

Prep Time: 10 minutes | Cook Time: 15 minutes | Serves: 4

1½ pounds filet mignon
2 tablespoons soy sauce
2 tablespoons butter, melted
1 teaspoon mustard powder
1 teaspoon garlic powder
Sea salt and ground black pepper, to taste

1. Toss the filet mignon with the remaining ingredients. Transfer the filet to the Crisper Tray. 2. Move SmartSwitch to AIR FRY/STOVETOP, set the cooking temperature to 400 degrees F and the cooking time to 14 minutes. Flip the food halfway through. 3. Serve and enjoy.

Per Serving: Calories 241; Fat: 17.52g; Sodium: 539mg; Carbs: 9.84g; Fiber: 1.9g; Sugar: 3.56g; Protein: 10.72g

Corned Beef

Prep Time: 10 minutes | Cook Time: 70 minutes | Serves: 4

1½ pounds beef brisket
2 tablespoons olive oil
1 tablespoon smoked paprika
1 tablespoon English mustard powder
1 teaspoon ground
1 teaspoon chili pepper flakes
2 garlic cloves, pressed

1. Toss the beef with the remaining ingredients. Transfer the food to the Crisper Tray. 2. Move SmartSwitch to AIR FRY/STOVETOP, set the cooking temperature to 390 degrees F and the cooking time to 15 minutes. 3. Flip the food when the cooking time is up, and then resume cooking them at 360 degrees F for 55 minutes more. Serve and enjoy.
Per Serving: Calories 241; Fat: 17.52g; Sodium: 539mg; Carbs: 9.84g; Fiber: 1.9g; Sugar: 3.56g; Protein: 10.72g

Onion Beef Shoulder

Prep Time: 10 minutes | Cook Time: 55 minutes | Serves: 4

1½ pounds beef shoulder
Sea salt and ground black pepper, to taste
1 teaspoon cayenne pepper
½ teaspoon ground cumin
2 tablespoons olive oil
2 cloves garlic, minced
1 teaspoon Dijon mustard
1 onion, cut into slices

1. Toss the beef with the spices, garlic, mustard, and olive oil. Transfer the food to the Crisper Tray. 2. Move SmartSwitch to AIR FRY/STOVETOP, set the cooking temperature to 390 degrees F and the cooking time to 45 minutes. 3. Flip the food halfway through. When the cooking time is up, add the onion and cook them for 10 minutes more. 4. Serve and enjoy.
Per Serving: Calories 241; Fat: 17.52g; Sodium: 539mg; Carbs: 9.84g; Fiber: 1.9g; Sugar: 3.56g; Protein: 10.72g

Roast Beef with Carrots

Prep Time: 15 minutes | Cook Time: 55 minutes | Serves: 5

2 pounds top sirloin roast
2 tablespoons olive oil
Sea salt and ground black pepper, to taste
2 carrots, sliced
1 tablespoon fresh coriander
1 tablespoon fresh thyme
1 tablespoon fresh rosemary

1. Toss the beef with the olive oil, salt, and black pepper. Transfer the food to the Crisper Tray. 2. Move SmartSwitch to AIR FRY/STOVETOP, set the cooking temperature to 390 degrees F and the cooking time to 55 minutes. Flip the beef after 27 minutes of cooking time. 3. Top the beef with the carrots and herbs when there are 10 minutes of cooking time left. Serve warm.
Per Serving: Calories 241; Fat: 17.52g; Sodium: 539mg; Carbs: 9.84g; Fiber: 1.9g; Sugar: 3.56g; Protein: 10.72g

Mushrooms Beef

Prep Time: 3 hourd | Cook Time: 10 minutes | Serves: 1

6 oz. beef
¼ onion, diced
½ cup mushroom slices
2 tbsp. favorite marinade

1. Slice or cube the beef and put it in a bowl. Cover the meat with the marinade, place a layer of aluminum foil or saran wrap over the bowl, and place the bowl in the refrigerator for 3 hours. 2. Place the Crisper Tray in the bottom position. Add the meat to it along with the onion and mushrooms, and close the lid. Move SmartSwitch to AIR FRY/STOVETOP, set the cooking temperature to 350 degrees F and the cooking time to 10 minutes. 3. Serve hot.
Per Serving: Calories 339; Fat 18.97g; Sodium 706mg; Carbs 6.55g; Fiber 0.6g; Sugar 4.31g; Protein 36.26g

Butter Bacon Cookies

Prep Time: 10 minutes | Cook Time: 15 minutes | Serves: 6

½ cup coconut flour
1 egg
1 tablespoon cream
3 tablespoons butter
4-ounces bacon, chopped, cooked
1 teaspoon apple cider vinegar
1 teaspoon baking powder
⅓ teaspoon salt
½ cup almond flour

1. Beat the egg in a bowl and whisk it. Add the baking powder, cream, and apple cider vinegar. 2. Add the butter stirrin gently. Add the almond flour, coconut flour, and salt. 3. Sprinkle the mixture with chopped cooked bacon and knead the dough. 4 Make 6 medium-sized meatballs. Place the Crisper Tray in the bottom position. Add the meatballs to it and close the lid. Mov SmartSwitch to AIR FRY/STOVETOP, set the cooking temperature to 360 degrees F and the cooking time to 15 minutes.
Per Serving: Calories 141; Fat 13.52g; Sodium 492mg; Carbs 2.62g; Fiber 0.7g; Sugar 0.73g; Protein 3.81g

Turmeric Bacon Omelet

Prep Time: 10 minutes | Cook Time: 13 minutes | Serves: 6

6 eggs
1 teaspoon butter
4-ounces bacon
1 tablespoon dill, dried
½ teaspoon salt
½ teaspoon turmeric
¼ cup almond milk

1. In a bowl, whisk eggs, then add the almond milk. Add the turmeric, dried dill, salt and mix well. 2. Slice the bacon. 3. Plac the Crisper Tray in the bottom position. Add the bacon to it and close the lid. Move SmartSwitch to AIR FRY/STOVETO and then use the center front arrows to select BAKE/ROAST. 4. Set the cooking temperature to 350 degrees F and the cookin time to 13 minutes. 5. Turn the bacon over and pour the egg mixture on top after 5 minutes of cooking time. 6. When th omelet is cooked, transfer it to a plate and slice into servings. Serve warm.
Per Serving: Calories 136; Fat 10.69g; Sodium 546mg; Carbs 3.22g; Fiber 0.8g; Sugar 1.05g; Protein 7.81g

Chapter 5 Fish and Seafood Recipes

Tilapia Tender

Prep Time: 5 minutes | Cook Time: 20 minutes | Serves: 4

4 tilapia fillets, boneless
1 tablespoon ghee
1 tablespoon apple cider vinegar
1 teaspoon dried cilantro

1. Sprinkle the tilapia fillets with apple cider vinegar and dried cilantro. 2. Place the Crisper Tray in the bottom position. Ad the fillets and ghee to it and close the lid. 3. Move SmartSwitch to AIR FRY/STOVETOP, set the cooking temperature to 37 degrees F and the cooking time to 20 minutes. 4. Flip the fillets halfway through. Serve hot.
Per Serving: Calories 138; Fat 4.85g; Sodium 83mg; Carbs 0.04g; Fiber 0g; Sugar 0.02g; Protein 23.32g

Flavorful Cod Fillets

Prep Time: 5 minutes | Cook Time: 12 minutes | Serves: 4

1 pound cod fillet, chopped
1 teaspoon coconut oil
1 teaspoon chili flakes
½ teaspoon cayenne pepper
1 teaspoon dried cilantro
¼ teaspoon ground nutmeg

1. Rub the cod fillet with coconut oil, chili flakes, cayenne pepper, dried cilantro, and ground nutmeg. 2. Place the Crisper Tra in the bottom position. Add the fillets to it and close the lid. 3. Move SmartSwitch to AIR FRY/STOVETOP, set the cookir temperature to 365 degrees F and the cooking time to 12 minutes. 4. Flip the fillets halfway through. Serve hot.
Per Serving: Calories 342; Fat 21.73g; Sodium 575mg; Carbs 10.75g; Fiber 7.2g; Sugar 0.98g; Protein 26.21g

Old-Fashioned Salmon Salad

Prep Time: 5 minutes | Cook Time: 12 minutes | Serves: 4

1 pound salmon fillets
Sea salt and ground black pepper, to taste
2 tablespoons olive oil
2 garlic cloves, minced
1 bell pepper, sliced
1 shallot, chopped
½ cup Kalamata olives, pitted and sliced
½ lemon, juiced
1 teaspoon Aleppo pepper, minced

1. Toss the salmon fillets with the salt, black pepper, and olive oil. Transfer the food to the Crisper Tray. 2. Move SmartSwitc to AIR FRY/STOVETOP, set the cooking temperature to 380 degrees F and the cooking time to 12 minutes. Flip the foo halfway through. 3. Chop the salmon fillets using two forks and add them to a salad bowl; add in the remaining ingredients an toss to combine. 4. Enjoy.
Per Serving: Calories 241; Fat: 17.52g; Sodium: 539mg; Carbs: 9.84g; Fiber: 1.9g; Sugar: 3.56g; Protein: 10.72g

Greek Monkfish Pita

Prep Time: 10 minutes | Cook Time: 15 minutes | Serves: 4

1 pound monkfish fillets
1 tablespoon olive oil
Sea salt and ground black pepper, to taste
Sea salt and ground black pepper, to taste
1 teaspoon cayenne pepper
4 tablespoons coleslaw
1 avocado, pitted, peeled and diced
1 tablespoon fresh parsley, chopped
4 (6-½ inch) Greek pitas, warmed

1. Toss the fish fillets with the olive oil. Transfer the fillets to the Crisper Tray. 2. Move SmartSwitch to AIR FRY/STOVETO set the cooking temperature to 400 degrees F and the cooking time to 14 minutes. Flip the food halfway through. 3. Assembl your pitas with the chopped fish and remaining ingredients and serve warm.
Per Serving: Calories 241; Fat: 17.52g; Sodium: 539mg; Carbs: 9.84g; Fiber: 1.9g; Sugar: 3.56g; Protein: 10.72g

Lime Chopped Salmon

Prep Time: 5 minutes | Cook Time: 20 minutes | Serves: 4

1 pound salmon, chopped
1 tablespoon lime juice
1 teaspoon avocado oil
1 teaspoon lime zest, grated
¼ teaspoon ground nutmeg

1. Rub the salmon with lime juice, lime zest, ground nutmeg, avocado oil. 2. Place the Crisper Tray in the bottom position. Add the food to it and close the lid. 3. Move SmartSwitch to AIR FRY/STOVETOP, set the cooking temperature to 360 degrees F and the cooking time to 20 minutes. 4. Serve hot.
Per Serving: Calories 185; Fat 9.31g; Sodium 491mg; Carbs 0.5g; Fiber 0.1g; Sugar 0.09g; Protein 23.42g

Coconut Nuggets

Prep Time: 10 minutes | Cook Time: 10 minutes | Serves: 4

¼ cup coconut shred
3 tablespoons almond flour
1 teaspoon salt
3 eggs, beaten
10 oz. cod fillet
1 teaspoon avocado oil

1. Cut the cod fillets into nuggets and sprinkle with salt. 2. Dip the fish in eggs and coat in almond flour. 3. After this, dip the fish in the eggs again and coat in the coconut shred. 4. Place the Crisper Tray in the bottom position. Add the nuggets to it, sprinkle them with avocado oil and close the lid. 5. Move SmartSwitch to AIR FRY/STOVETOP, set the cooking temperature to 375 degrees F and the cooking time to 10 minutes. 6. Flip the fillets halfway through. Serve hot.
Per Serving: Calories 114; Fat 5.03g; Sodium 859mg; Carbs 0.99g; Fiber 0.3g; Sugar 0.55g; Protein 15.27g

Mustard Tilapia Fillets

Prep Time: 10 minutes | Cook Time: 14 minutes | Serves: 4

1 cup Monterey Jack cheese, grated
4 tilapia fillets
¼ teaspoon ground cumin
1 tablespoon Dijon mustard

1. Rub the tilapia fillets with ground cumin and Dijon mustard. 2. Place the Crisper Tray in the bottom position. Add the fillets to it and top them with cheese, and then close the lid. 3. Move SmartSwitch to AIR FRY/STOVETOP, set the cooking temperature to 370 degrees F and the cooking time to 14 minutes. 4. Serve hot.
Per Serving: Calories 237; Fat 12.12g; Sodium 302mg; Carbs 0.51g; Fiber 0.2g; Sugar 0.2g; Protein 31.54g

Famous Fish Sticks

Prep Time: 5 minutes | Cook Time: 10 minutes | Serves: 4

½ cup all-purpose flour
1 large egg
2 tablespoons buttermilk
½ cup crackers, crushed
1 teaspoon garlic powder
Sea salt and ground black pepper, to taste
½ teaspoon cayenne pepper
1 pound tilapia fillets, cut into strips

1. In a shallow bowl, place the flour. Whisk the egg and buttermilk in a second bowl, and mix the crushed crackers and spices in a third bowl. 2. Dip the fish strips in the flour mixture, then in the whisked eggs; finally, roll the fish strips over the cracker mixture until they are well coated on all sides. 3. Transfer the fish sticks to the Crisper Tray. Move SmartSwitch to AIR FRY/STOVETOP, set the cooking temperature to 400 degrees F and the cooking time to 10 minutes. 4. Flip the food halfway through. Serve and enjoy.
Per Serving: Calories 241; Fat: 17.52g; Sodium: 539mg; Carbs: 9.84g; Fiber: 1.9g; Sugar: 3.56g; Protein: 10.72g

Spicy Squid Pieces

Prep Time: 5 minutes | Cook Time: 5 minutes | Serves: 5

1½ pounds squid, cut into pieces
1 chili pepper, chopped
1 small lemon, squeezed
2 tablespoons olive oil
1 tablespoon capers, drained
2 garlic cloves, minced
1 tablespoon coriander, chopped
2 tablespoons parsley, chopped
1 teaspoon sweet paprika
Sea salt and ground black pepper, to taste

1. Toss all ingredients. Transfer the food to the Crisper Tray. 2. Move SmartSwitch to AIR FRY/STOVETOP, set the cooking temperature to 400 degrees F and the cooking time to 5 minutes. 3. Flip the food halfway through. Serve and enjoy.
Per Serving: Calories 241; Fat: 17.52g; Sodium: 539mg; Carbs: 9.84g; Fiber: 1.9g; Sugar: 3.56g; Protein: 10.72g

Peppercorn Halibut Steaks

Prep Time: 10 minutes | Cook Time: 15 minutes | Serves: 4

1 pound halibut steaks
¼ cup butter
Sea salt, to taste
2 tablespoons fresh chives, chopped
1 teaspoon garlic, minced
1 teaspoon mixed peppercorns, ground

1. Toss the halibut steaks with the rest of the ingredients. Transfer the food to the Crisper Tray. 2. Move SmartSwitch to AIR FRY/STOVETOP, set the cooking temperature to 400 degrees F and the cooking time to 12 minutes. Flip the food halfway through. 3. Serve and enjoy.
Per Serving: Calories 241; Fat: 17.52g; Sodium: 539mg; Carbs: 9.84g; Fiber: 1.9g; Sugar: 3.56g; Protein: 10.72g

Delicious Fried Calamari

Prep Time: 5 minutes | Cook Time: 5 minutes | Serves: 4

1 cup all-purpose flour
½ cup tortilla chips, crushed
1 teaspoon mustard powder
1 tablespoon dried parsley
Sea salt and freshly ground black pepper, to taste
1 teaspoon cayenne pepper
2 tablespoons olive oil
1 pound calamari, sliced into rings

1. In a mixing bowl, thoroughly combine the flour, tortilla chips, spices, and olive oil. Dip the calamari into the flour mixture to coat. Transfer the food to the Crisper Tray. 2. Move SmartSwitch to AIR FRY/STOVETOP, set the cooking temperature to 400 degrees F and the cooking time to 5 minutes. Flip the food halfway through. 3. Serve and enjoy.
Per Serving: Calories 241; Fat: 17.52g; Sodium: 539mg; Carbs: 9.84g; Fiber: 1.9g; Sugar: 3.56g; Protein: 10.72g

Exotic Prawns

Prep Time: 5 minutes | Cook Time: 10 minutes | Serves: 4

1½ pounds prawns, peeled and deveined
2 garlic cloves, minced
2 tablespoons fresh chives, chopped
½ cup whole-wheat flour
½ teaspoon sweet paprika
1 teaspoon hot paprika
Salt and freshly ground black pepper, to taste
2 tablespoons coconut oil
2 tablespoons lemon juice

1. Toss all ingredients. Transfer the prawns to the Crisper Tray. 2. Move SmartSwitch to AIR FRY/STOVETOP, set the cooking temperature to 400 degrees F and the cooking time to 9 minutes. Flip the food halfway through. 3. Serve and enjoy.
Per Serving: Calories 241; Fat: 17.52g; Sodium: 539mg; Carbs: 9.84g; Fiber: 1.9g; Sugar: 3.56g; Protein: 10.72g

Chimichurri Mackerel Fillets

Prep Time: 10 minutes | Cook Time: 15 minutes | Serves: 4

1 tablespoon olive oil, or more to taste
1½ pounds mackerel fillets
Sea salt and ground black pepper, taste
2 tablespoons parsley
2 garlic cloves, minced
2 tablespoons fresh lime juice

1. Toss the fish fillets with the remaining ingredients. Transfer the fillets to the Crisper Tray. 2. Move SmartSwitch to AIR FRY/STOVETOP, set the cooking temperature to 400 degrees F and the cooking time to 14 minutes. Flip the food halfway through. 3. Serve and enjoy.
Per Serving: Calories 241; Fat: 17.52g; Sodium: 539mg; Carbs: 9.84g; Fiber: 1.9g; Sugar: 3.56g; Protein: 10.72g

Simple-Seasoned Shrimps

Prep Time: 10 minutes | Cook Time: 5 minutes | Serves: 3

1 pound shrimps, peeled
1 teaspoon onion powder
1 teaspoon avocado oil
½ teaspoon salt

1. Sprinkle the shrimps with onion powder, avocado oil, and salt. 2. Place the Crisper Tray in the bottom position. Place the shrimps on the tray and close the lid. 3. Move SmartSwitch to AIR FRY/STOVETOP, and then use the center front arrows to select BAKE/ROAST. Set the cooking temperature to 400 degrees F and the cooking time to 5 minutes. 4. Serve and enjoy.
Per Serving: Calories 145; Fat 2.28g; Sodium 568mg; Carbs 0.63g; Fiber 0.1g; Sugar 0.05g; Protein 30.47g

Cheddar Cod Fillets

Prep Time: 10 minutes | Cook Time: 15 minutes | Serves: 4

4 cod fillets, boneless
1 cup Cheddar cheese, shredded
1 teaspoon avocado oil
½ teaspoon ground black pepper

1. Sprinkle the cod fillets with avocado oil and rub with ground black pepper. Place the Crisper Tray in the bottom position. 2. Add the food to it and top them with Cheddar cheese and close the lid. Move SmartSwitch to AIR FRY/STOVETOP, set the cooking temperature to 370 degrees F and the cooking time to 15 minutes. 3. Serve warm.
Per Serving: Calories 225; Fat 12.77g; Sodium 564mg; Carbs 0.63g; Fiber 0.1g; Sugar 0.09g; Protein 25.68g

Boneless Cod in Sauce

Prep Time: 5 minutes | Cook Time: 15 minutes | Serves: 2

2 cod fillets, boneless
¼ cup heavy cream
1 teaspoon ground black pepper
1 teaspoon garlic powder
1 teaspoon butter, softened
½ teaspoon cayenne pepper

1. In the mixing bowl, mix heavy cream, ground black pepper, garlic powder, and cayenne pepper. 2. Add butter and whisk the mixture. Place the Crisper Tray in the bottom position. 3. Add the cod fillets to it and top them with heavy cream sauce and close the lid. Move SmartSwitch to AIR FRY/STOVETOP, set the cooking temperature to 375 degrees F and the cooking time to 15 minutes. 4. Serve warm.
Per Serving: Calories 159; Fat 8.07g; Sodium 374mg; Carbs 2.73g; Fiber 0.6g; Sugar 0.51g; Protein 18.5g

Tilapia Nuggets

Prep Time: 15 minutes | Cook Time: 10 minutes | Serves: 4

1½ pounds tilapia fillets, cut into 1 ½-inch pieces
1 tablespoon dried thyme
1 tablespoon dried oregano
1 tablespoon Dijon mustard
2 tablespoons olive oil
1½ cups all-purpose flour
Sea salt and ground black pepper, to taste
½ teaspoon baking powder

1. Pat the fish dry with kitchen towels. In a mixing bowl, thoroughly combine all remaining ingredients until well mixed Dip the fish pieces into the batter to coat. 2. Transfer the fillet pieces to the Crisper Tray. Move SmartSwitch to AIR FRY STOVETOP, set the cooking temperature to 400 degrees F and the cooking time to 10 minutes. 3. Flip the food halfway through. Serve and enjoy.

Per Serving: Calories 241; Fat: 17.52g; Sodium: 539mg; Carbs: 9.84g; Fiber: 1.9g; Sugar: 3.56g; Protein: 10.72g

Cilantro Swordfish Steaks

Prep Time: 10 minutes | Cook Time: 15 minutes | Serves: 4

1 pound swordfish steaks
4 garlic cloves, peeled
4 tablespoons olive oil
2 tablespoons fresh lemon juice, more for later
1 tablespoon fresh cilantro, roughly chopped
1 teaspoon Spanish paprika
Sea salt and ground black pepper, to taste

1. Toss the swordfish steaks with the remaining ingredients. Transfer the steaks to the Crisper Tray. 2. Move SmartSwitch to AIR FRY/STOVETOP, set the cooking temperature to 400 degrees F and the cooking time to 10 minutes. Flip the food halfway through. 3. Serve and enjoy.

Per Serving: Calories 241; Fat: 17.52g; Sodium: 539mg; Carbs: 9.84g; Fiber: 1.9g; Sugar: 3.56g; Protein: 10.72g

Salmon with Lemon Zest

Prep Time: 10 minutes | Cook Time: 20 minutes | Serves: 4

1 pound salmon fillets, boneless
2 tablespoons lemon juice
1 teaspoon lemon zest, grated
1 teaspoon avocado oil

1. Mix lemon juice with lemon zest, and avocado oil. Carefully rub the salmon fillets with lemon mixture. 2. Place the Crisper Tray in the elevated position. Add the salmon fillets to it and close the lid. 3. Move SmartSwitch to RAPID COOKER, and then use the center front arrows to select Steam & Crisp. Set the cooking temperature to 360 degrees F and the cooking time to 10 minutes. 4. Serve warm.

Per Serving: Calories 148; Fat 5.42g; Sodium 57mg; Carbs 0.61g; Fiber 0g; Sugar 0.22g; Protein 22.87g

Bacon & Scallops

Prep Time: 15 minutes | Cook Time: 7 minutes | Serves: 4

1 pound scallops
4 oz. bacon, sliced
1 teaspoon avocado oil
1 teaspoon chili powder

1. Wrap the scallops in the bacon and sprinkle with avocado oil and chili powder. 2. Place the Crisper Tray in the bottom position. Add the food to it and close the lid. Move SmartSwitch to AIR FRY/STOVETOP, set the cooking temperature to 400 degrees F and the cooking time to 7 minutes. 3. Serve warm.

Per Serving: Calories 178; Fat 10.15g; Sodium 879mg; Carbs 5.73g; Fiber 1g; Sugar 0.05g; Protein 16.79g

Garlicky Salmon Cubes

Prep Time: 5 minutes | Cook Time: 15 minutes | Serves: 4

2-pounds salmon, cubed
1 teaspoon minced garlic
½ teaspoon garlic powder
1 tablespoon ghee, melted
½ teaspoon dried dill
½ teaspoon dried parsley

1. Mix salmon cubes with minced garlic, garlic powder, dried dill, and parsley. 2. Place the Crisper Tray in the bottom position. Add the ghee and salmon cubes to it and close the lid. Move SmartSwitch to AIR FRY/STOVETOP, set the cooking temperature to 370 degrees F and the cooking time to 15 minutes. 3. Flip the fish every 5 minutes during cooking. Serve hot.
Per Serving: Calories 317; Fat 12.91g; Sodium 193mg; Carbs 0.69g; Fiber 0.1g; Sugar 0.02g; Protein 46.68g

Chili Diced Cod

Prep Time: 15 minutes | Cook Time: 10 minutes | Serves: 2

1 chili pepper, chopped
12 oz. cod fillet, sliced
1 teaspoon avocado oil
½ teaspoon ground cinnamon

1. Sprinkle the cod fillet with avocado oil and put it in the Crisper Tray, and then top it with chili pepper and ground cinnamon. 2. Close the lid. Move SmartSwitch to AIR FRY/STOVETOP, set the cooking temperature to 375 degrees F and the cooking time to 9 minutes. 3. Serve hot.
Per Serving: Calories 148; Fat 3g; Sodium 517mg; Carbs 2.65g; Fiber 0.7g; Sugar 1.16g; Protein 26.45g

Delectable Swordfish Steaks

Prep Time: 10 minutes | Cook Time: 15 minutes | Serves: 4

1 pound swordfish steaks
2 tablespoons olive oil
2 teaspoons tamari sauce
Salt and freshly ground pepper, to taste
¼ cup dry red wine
2 sprigs rosemary
1 sprig thyme
1 tablespoon grated lemon rind

1. Toss the swordfish steaks with the remaining ingredients in a ceramic dish; cover and let it marinate in your refrigerator for about 2 hours. Discard the marinade and place the fish on the Crisper Tray. 2. Move SmartSwitch to AIR FRY/STOVETOP, set the cooking temperature to 400 degrees F and the cooking time to 10 minutes. 3. Flip the food halfway through. Serve and enjoy.
Per Serving: Calories 241; Fat: 17.52g; Sodium: 539mg; Carbs: 9.84g; Fiber: 1.9g; Sugar: 3.56g; Protein: 10.72g

Simple Shrimps

Prep Time: 5 minutes | Cook Time: 2 minutes | Serves: 4

1 tablespoon avocado oil
½ teaspoon salt
1 teaspoon dried basil
1 pound shrimps, peeled

1. Mix shrimps with salt, dried basil, and avocado oil. 2. Place the Crisper Tray in the bottom position. Add the food to it and close the lid. 3. Move SmartSwitch to AIR FRY/STOVETOP, set the cooking temperature to 365 degrees F and the cooking time to 12 minutes. 4. Serve hot.
Per Serving: Calories 128; Fat 4.09g; Sodium 426mg; Carbs 0.08g; Fiber 0.1g; Sugar 0g; Protein 22.83g

Calamari in Sherry Wine

Prep Time: 5 minutes | Cook Time: 5 minutes | Serves: 4

1 pound calamari, sliced into rings
2 tablespoons butter, melted
4 garlic cloves, smashed
2 tablespoons sherry wine
2 tablespoons fresh lemon juice
Coarse sea salt and ground black pepper, to taste
1 teaspoon paprika
1 teaspoon dried oregano

1. Toss all ingredients in a bowl. Transfer the food to the Crisper Tray. 2. Move SmartSwitch to AIR FRY/STOVETOP, set th cooking temperature to 400 degrees F and the cooking time to 5 minutes. 3. Flip the food halfway through. Serve and enjoy.
Per Serving: Calories 241; Fat: 17.52g; Sodium: 539mg; Carbs: 9.84g; Fiber: 1.9g; Sugar: 3.56g; Protein: 10.72g

Lemon Broccoli & Shrimp

Prep Time: 5 minutes | Cook Time: 10 minutes | Serves: 4

1 pound raw shrimp, peeled and deveined
½ pound broccoli florets
1 tablespoon olive oil
1 garlic clove, minced
2 tablespoons freshly squeezed lemon juice
Coarse sea salt and ground black pepper, to taste
1 teaspoon paprika

1. Toss all ingredients. Transfer the shrimp and broccoli to the Crisper Tray. 2. Move SmartSwitch to AIR FRY/STOVETOP set the cooking temperature to 400 degrees F and the cooking time to 6 minutes. 3. Flip the food halfway through. Serve an enjoy.
Per Serving: Calories 241; Fat: 17.52g; Sodium: 539mg; Carbs: 9.84g; Fiber: 1.9g; Sugar: 3.56g; Protein: 10.72g

Homemade Prawn Salad

Prep Time: 10 minutes | Cook Time: 6 minutes | Serves: 4

1½ pounds king prawns, peeled and deveined
Coarse sea salt and ground black pepper, to taste
1 tablespoon fresh lemon juice
1 cup mayonnaise
1 teaspoon Dijon mustard
1 tablespoon fresh parsley, roughly chopped
1 teaspoon fresh dill, minced
1 shallot, chopped

1. Toss the prawns with the salt and black pepper. Transfer the prawns to the Crisper Tray. 2. Move SmartSwitch to AIR FRY STOVETOP, set the cooking temperature to 400 degrees F and the cooking time to 6 minutes. Flip the food halfway through. 3 Add the prawns to a salad bowl; add in the remaining ingredients and stir to combine well. Enjoy.
Per Serving: Calories 241; Fat: 17.52g; Sodium: 539mg; Carbs: 9.84g; Fiber: 1.9g; Sugar: 3.56g; Protein: 10.72g

Crispy Fish Fingers

Prep Time: 10 minutes | Cook Time: 10 minutes | Serves: 4

2 eggs
¼ cup all-purpose flour
Sea salt and ground black pepper, to taste
½ teaspoon onion powder
¼ teaspoon garlic powder
¼ cup plain breadcrumbs
1½ tablespoons olive oil
1 pound cod fish fillets, slice into pieces

1. In a mixing bowl, thoroughly combine the eggs, flour, and spices. In a separate bowl, thoroughly combine the breadcrumb and olive oil. 2. Dip the fish pieces into the flour mixture to coat; roll the fish pieces over the breadcrumb mixture until they ar well coated on all sides. 3. Transfer the fish pieces to the Crisper Tray. Move SmartSwitch to AIR FRY/STOVETOP, set th cooking temperature to 400 degrees F and the cooking time to 10 minutes. 4. Flip the food halfway through. Serve and enjoy.
Per Serving: Calories 241; Fat: 17.52g; Sodium: 539mg; Carbs: 9.84g; Fiber: 1.9g; Sugar: 3.56g; Protein: 10.72g

Muffin Tuna Melts

Prep Time: 10 minutes | Cook Time: 15 minutes | Serves: 4

1 pound tuna, boneless and chopped
½ cup all-purpose flour
½ cup breadcrumbs
2 tablespoons buttermilk
2 eggs, whisked
Kosher salt and ground black pepper, to taste
½ teaspoon cayenne pepper
1 tablespoon olive oil
4 mozzarella cheese slices
4 English muffins

1. Mix all ingredients, except for the cheese and English muffins, in a bowl. Shape the mixture into four patties. Transfer the patties to the Crisper Tray. 2. Move SmartSwitch to AIR FRY/STOVETOP, set the cooking temperature to 400 degrees F and the cooking time to 14 minutes. Flip the food halfway through. 3. Place the cheese slices on the warm patties and serve on hamburger buns and enjoy!

Per Serving: Calories 241; Fat: 17.52g; Sodium: 539mg; Carbs: 9.84g; Fiber: 1.9g; Sugar: 3.56g; Protein: 10.72g

Lemon Mahi-Mahi Fillets

Prep Time: 10 minutes | Cook Time: 15 minutes | Serves: 4

1 pound mahi-mahi fillets
2 tablespoons butter, at room temperature
2 tablespoons fresh lemon juice
Kosher salt and freshly ground black pepper, to taste
1 teaspoon smoked paprika
1 teaspoon garlic, minced
1 teaspoon dried basil
1 teaspoon dried oregano

1. Toss the fish fillets with the remaining ingredients. Transfer the fillets to the Crisper Tray. 2. Move SmartSwitch to AIR FRY/STOVETOP, set the cooking temperature to 400 degrees F and the cooking time to 14 minutes. 3. Flip the food halfway through. Serve and enjoy.

Per Serving: Calories 241; Fat: 17.52g; Sodium: 539mg; Carbs: 9.84g; Fiber: 1.9g; Sugar: 3.56g; Protein: 10.72g

Typical Fish Tacos

Prep Time: 10 minutes | Cook Time: 15 minutes | Serves: 4

1 pound codfish fillets
1 tablespoon olive oil
1 avocado, pitted, peeled and mashed
4 tablespoons mayonnaise
1 teaspoon mustard
1 shallot, chopped
1 habanero pepper, chopped
8 small corn tortillas

1. Toss the fish fillets with the olive oil; place them in a lightly oiled Air Fryer cooking basket. 2. Cook the fish fillets at 400 degrees F for about 14 minutes, turning them over halfway through the cooking time. 3. Assemble your tacos with the chopped fish and remaining ingredients and serve warm. Bon appétit!

Per Serving: Calories 241; Fat: 17.52g; Sodium: 539mg; Carbs: 9.84g; Fiber: 1.9g; Sugar: 3.56g; Protein: 10.72g

Savory Shrimp

Prep Time: 10 minutes | Cook Time: 6 minutes | Serves: 4

1½ pounds raw shrimp, peeled and deveined
1 tablespoon olive oil
1 teaspoon garlic, minced
1 teaspoon cayenne pepper
½ teaspoon lemon pepper
Sea salt, to taste

1. Toss all ingredients. Transfer the shrimp to the Crisper Tray. 2. Move SmartSwitch to AIR FRY/STOVETOP, set the cooking temperature to 400 degrees F and the cooking time to 6 minutes. Flip the food halfway through. 3. Serve and enjoy.

Per Serving: Calories 241; Fat: 17.52g; Sodium: 539mg; Carbs: 9.84g; Fiber: 1.9g; Sugar: 3.56g; Protein: 10.72g

Easy-to-Make Salmon

Prep Time: 10 minutes | Cook Time: 9 minutes | Serves: 3

1 pound salmon
1 teaspoon dried rosemary
2 tablespoons olive oil
½ teaspoon salt

1. Sprinkle the salmon with dried rosemary, olive oil, and salt. 2. Place the Crisper Tray in the bottom position. Add the salmo to it and close the lid. 3. Move SmartSwitch to AIR FRY/STOVETOP, set the cooking temperature to 390 degrees F and th cooking time to 9 minutes. 4. Serve hot.

Per Serving: Calories 272; Fat 15.67g; Sodium 501mg; Carbs 0.05g; Fiber 0g; Sugar 0g; Protein 31g

Cumin Catfish Fillets

Prep Time: 5 minutes | Cook Time: 15 minutes | Serves: 4

1 tablespoon ground cumin
1 tablespoon avocado oil
½ teaspoon apple cider vinegar
1 pound catfish fillet

1. Rub the catfish fillet with ground cumin, avocado oil, and apple cider vinegar. Place the Crisper Tray in the bottom position. 2 Add the fillet to it and close the lid. Move SmartSwitch to AIR FRY/STOVETOP, set the cooking temperature to 360 degree F and the cooking time to 15 minutes. 3. Serve hot.

Per Serving: Calories 145; Fat 7.03g; Sodium 51mg; Carbs 0.74g; Fiber 0.2g; Sugar 0.1g; Protein 18.84g

Orange Roughy Fillets

Prep Time: 5 minutes | Cook Time: 10 minutes | Serves: 4

1 pound orange roughy fillets
2 tablespoons butter
2 cloves garlic, minced
Sea salt and red pepper flakes, to taste

1. Toss the fish fillets with the remaining ingredients. Transfer the fillets to the Crisper Tray. 2. Move SmartSwitch to AI FRY/STOVETOP, set the cooking temperature to 400 degrees F and the cooking time to 10 minutes. Flip the food halfwa through. 3. Serve and enjoy.

Per Serving: Calories 241; Fat: 17.52g; Sodium: 539mg; Carbs: 9.84g; Fiber: 1.9g; Sugar: 3.56g; Protein: 10.72g

Jalapeno Shrimp Vinaigrette

Prep Time: 5 minutes | Cook Time: 2 minutes | Serves: 4

1 pound shrimps, peeled
3 tablespoons apple cider vinegar
1 teaspoon ground black pepper
1 teaspoon dried dill
1 jalapeno, chopped
1 tablespoon avocado oil

1. Mix shrimps with all remaining ingredients. Place the Crisper Tray in the bottom position. 2. Add the food to it and clos the lid. Move SmartSwitch to AIR FRY/STOVETOP, set the cooking temperature to 350 degrees F and the cooking time to 1 minutes. 3. Serve hot.

Per Serving: Calories 134; Fat 4.19g; Sodium 136mg; Carbs 1.08g; Fiber 0.4g; Sugar 0.19g; Protein 22.98g

Turmeric Tilapia Fillets

Prep Time: 5 minutes | Cook Time: 20 minutes | Serves: 4

4 tilapia fillets, boneless and halved
1 tablespoon avocado oil
1 teaspoon ground turmeric

1. Sprinkle the tilapia fillets with avocado oil and ground turmeric. 2. Place the Crisper Tray in the bottom position. Place the fillets on the tray and close the lid. 3. Move SmartSwitch to AIR FRY/STOVETOP, and then use the center front arrows to select BAKE/ROAST. 4. Set the cooking temperature to 350 degrees F and the cooking time to 20 minutes. Flip the fillets halfway through. 5. Serve and enjoy.

Per Serving: Calories 145; Fat 5.5g; Sodium 61mg; Carbs 0.5g; Fiber 0.2g; Sugar 0.02g; Protein 23.37g

Cilantro Shrimp

Prep Time: 5 minutes | Cook Time: 12 minutes | Serves: 4

1 pound shrimp, peeled and deveined
1 teaspoon dried parsley
1 teaspoon dried cilantro
1 tablespoon olive oil
½ teaspoon salt

Mix parsley with shrimps, cilantro, salt, and olive oil. Place the Crisper Tray in the bottom position. 2. Add the food to it and close the lid. Move SmartSwitch to AIR FRY/STOVETOP, set the cooking temperature to 360 degrees F and the cooking time to 12 minutes. 3. Serve hot.

Per Serving: Calories 126; Fat 3.96g; Sodium 426mg; Carbs 0.02g; Fiber 0g; Sugar 0g; Protein 22.8g

Allspices Salmon

Prep Time: 10 minutes | Cook Time: 15 minutes | Serves: 4

1 teaspoon allspices
1 pound salmon
1 tablespoon avocado oil

1. Rub the salmon with allspices and sprinkle with avocado oil. 2. Place the Crisper Tray in the bottom position. Add the salmon to it and close the lid. 3. Move SmartSwitch to AIR FRY/STOVETOP, set the cooking temperature to 360 degrees F and the cooking time to 15 minutes. 4. Serve hot.

Per Serving: Calories 206; Fat 11.67g; Sodium 491mg; Carbs 0.34g; Fiber 0.1g; Sugar 0g; Protein 23.42g

Aminos Cod

Prep Time: 10 minutes | Cook Time: 9 minutes | Serves: 6

2-pound salmon fillet, chopped
1 teaspoon Erythritol
1 tablespoon coconut aminos
½ teaspoon dried basil
1 tablespoon avocado oil

1. Mix salmon with Erythritol, coconut aminos, dried basil, and avocado oil. Marinate the fish for 5 minutes. 2. Place the Crisper Tray in the bottom position. Add the fillet with the marinade to it and close the lid. 3. Move SmartSwitch to AIR FRY/STOVETOP, set the cooking temperature to 360 degrees F and the cooking time to 9 minutes. 4. Serve hot.

Per Serving: Calories 203; Fat 8.04g; Sodium 78mg; Carbs 0.12g; Fiber 0.1g; Sugar 0.07g; Protein 30.49g

Chapter 6 Snack and Appetizer Recipes

Sweet Potato Chips

Prep Time: 5 minutes | Cook Time: 15 minutes | Serves: 3

2 large-sized sweet potatoes, peeled and cut into thin slices
2 teaspoons butter, melted
Sea salt and ground black pepper, to taste
½ teaspoon dried oregano
½ teaspoon dried basil
½ teaspoon dried rosemary

1. Toss the sweet potato with the remaining ingredients. 2. Place the Crisper Tray in the bottom position. Add the food to it and close the lid. 3. Move SmartSwitch to AIR FRY/STOVETOP, set the cooking temperature to 360 degrees F and the cooking time to 14 minutes. 4. Toss the potato chips halfway through. Serve hot.

Per Serving: Calories 134; Fat 2.79g; Sodium 64mg; Carbs 25.55g; Fiber 4.3g; Sugar 7.79g; Protein 2.57g

Coated Onion Rings

Prep Time: 5 minutes | Cook Time: 8 minutes | Serves: 4

1 cup all-purpose flour
Sea salt and black pepper, to taste
1 teaspoon red pepper flakes, crushed
½ teaspoon cumin powder
1 egg
1 cup breadcrumbs
1 medium yellow onion, sliced

1. In a shallow bowl, mix the flour, salt, black pepper, red pepper flakes, and cumin powder. 2. Whisk the egg in another shallow bowl. Place the breadcrumbs in a separate bowl. 3. Dip the onion rings in the flour, then in the eggs, then in the breadcrumbs. 4. Place the Crisper Tray in the bottom position. Add the food to it and close the lid. Move SmartSwitch to AIR FRY/STOVETOP, set the cooking temperature to 380 degrees F and the cooking time to 8 minutes. 5. Serve hot.

Per Serving: Calories 134; Fat 1.45g; Sodium 21mg; Carbs 24.73g; Fiber 1g; Sugar 0.3g; Protein 4.77g

Jalapeno Bacon Poppers

Prep Time: 5 minutes | Cook Time: 7 minutes | Serves: 4

4 ounces Cottage cheese, crumbled
4 ounces cheddar cheese, shredded
1 teaspoon mustard seeds
8 jalapenos, seeded and sliced in half lengthwise
8 slices bacon, sliced in half lengthwise

1. Thoroughly combine the cheese and mustard seeds. 2. Spoon the mixture into the jalapeno halves. Wrap each jalapeno with half a slice of bacon and secure with toothpicks. 3. Place the Crisper Tray in the bottom position. Add the jalapeno poppers to it and close the lid. Move SmartSwitch to AIR FRY/STOVETOP, set the cooking temperature to 320 degrees F and the cooking time to 7 minutes. 4. Serve hot.

Per Serving: Calories 300; Fat 24.44g; Sodium 661mg; Carbs 6.39g; Fiber 0.8g; Sugar 4.38g; Protein 13.86g

Bacon-Wrapped Jalapeño Poppers

Prep Time: 10 minutes | Cook Time: 15 minutes | Serves: 6

6 large jalapeños
4 ounces ⅓-less-fat cream cheese
¼ cup (1 ounce) shredded reduced-fat sharp cheddar cheese*
2 scallions, green tops only, sliced
6 slices center-cut bacon, halved

1. Wearing rubber gloves, halve the jalapeños lengthwise to make 12 pieces. Scoop out the seeds and membranes and discard. 2. In a medium bowl, combine the cream cheese, cheddar, and scallions. Using a small spoon or spatula, fill the jalapeños with the cream cheese filling. 3. Wrap a bacon strip around each pepper and secure with a toothpick. Transfer the stuffed peppers to the Crisper Tray. 4. Move SmartSwitch to AIR FRY/STOVETOP, set the cooking temperature to 325 degrees F and the cooking time to 12 minutes. 5. When cooked, the peppers should be tender, the bacon should be browned and crisp, and the cheese should be melted. 6. Serve warm.

Per Serving: Calories 241; Fat: 17.52g; Sodium: 539mg; Carbs: 9.84g; Fiber: 1.9g; Sugar: 3.56g; Protein: 10.72g

Tasty Chicken Wings

Prep Time: 5 minutes | Cook Time: 18 minutes | Serves: 3

¾ pound chicken wings
1 tablespoon olive oil
1 teaspoon mustard seeds
1 teaspoon cayenne pepper
1 teaspoon garlic powder
Sea salt and ground black pepper, to taste

1. Toss the chicken wings with the remaining ingredients. Place the Crisper Tray in the bottom position. 2. Add the chicke wings to it and close the lid. Move SmartSwitch to AIR FRY/STOVETOP, set the cooking temperature to 380 degrees F an the cooking time to 18 minutes. 3. Flip the wings halfway through. Serve hot.
Per Serving: Calories 193; Fat 8.89g; Sodium 93mg; Carbs 1.77g; Fiber 0.5g; Sugar 0.14g; Protein 25.41g

Breaded Cauliflower Florets

Prep Time: 5 minutes | Cook Time: 15 minutes | Serves: 4

2 eggs, whisked
1 cup breadcrumbs
Sea salt and ground black pepper, to taste
1 teaspoon cayenne pepper
1 teaspoon chili powder
½ teaspoon onion powder
½ teaspoon cumin powder
½ teaspoon garlic powder
1 pound cauliflower florets

1. Mix the eggs, breadcrumbs, and spices until well combined. 2. Dip the cauliflower florets in the batter. 3. Place the Crisp Tray in the bottom position. Add the cauliflower florets to it and close the lid. Move SmartSwitch to AIR FRY/STOVETOP, s the cooking temperature to 350 degrees F and the cooking time to 15 minutes. 4. Turn the food over halfway through. Serv hot.
Per Serving: Calories 178; Fat 4.1g; Sodium 284mg; Carbs 27.53g; Fiber 4.1g; Sugar 4.63g; Protein 9.06g

Sticky Brussels Sprouts

Prep Time: 5 minutes | Cook Time: 10 minutes | Serves: 4

1 pound Brussels sprouts, trimmed
2 tablespoons sesame oil
2 tablespoons agave syrup
2 tablespoons rice wine
1 teaspoon chili flakes
1 teaspoon garlic powder
½ teaspoon paprika
Sea salt and ground black pepper, to taste

1. Toss the Brussels sprouts with the remaining ingredients. Place the Crisper Tray in the bottom position. 2. Add the Brusse sprouts to it and close the lid. Move SmartSwitch to AIR FRY/STOVETOP, set the cooking temperature to 380 degrees F an the cooking time to 10 minutes. 3. Toss the food halfway through. Serve hot.
Per Serving: Calories 147; Fat 7.32g; Sodium 56mg; Carbs 20.1g; Fiber 4.9g; Sugar 11.12g; Protein 4.19g

Glazed Baby Carrot Halves

Prep Time: 5 minutes | Cook Time: 15 minutes | Serves: 3

¾ pound baby carrots, halved lengthwise
2 tablespoons coconut oil
½ teaspoon cumin powder
2 tablespoons honey
2 tablespoons white wine

1. Toss the carrots with the remaining ingredients. Place the Crisper Tray in the bottom position. 2. Add the carrots to it ar close the lid. Move SmartSwitch to AIR FRY/STOVETOP, set the cooking temperature to 380 degrees F and the cooking tin to 15 minutes. 3. Toss the food halfway through. Serve hot.
Per Serving: Calories 162; Fat 9.3g; Sodium 90mg; Carbs 21.15g; Fiber 3.4g; Sugar 17.01g; Protein 0.88g

Savory Potato Chips

Prep Time: 5 minutes | Cook Time: 16 minutes | Serves: 3

2 large-sized potatoes, thinly sliced
2 tablespoons olive oil
1 teaspoon Mediterranean herb mix
1 teaspoon cayenne pepper
Coarse sea salt and ground black pepper, to taste

1. Toss the potatoes with the remaining ingredients. 2. Place the Crisper Tray in the bottom position. Add the potatoes to it and close the lid. 3. Move SmartSwitch to AIR FRY/STOVETOP, set the cooking temperature to 360 degrees F and the cooking time to 16 minutes. 4. Toss the food halfway through. Serve hot.

Per Serving: Calories 273; Fat 9.35g; Sodium 16mg; Carbs 43.94g; Fiber 5.8g; Sugar 2.02g; Protein 5.12g

Mustard Broccoli Florets

Prep Time: 5 minutes | Cook Time: 10 minutes | Serves: 4

1 pound broccoli florets
2 tablespoons butter, room temperature
¼ teaspoon mustard seeds
1 tablespoon soy sauce
Sea salt and freshly ground black pepper, to taste

1. Toss all the ingredients in a bowl. Place the Crisper Tray in the bottom position. 2. Add the food to it and close the lid. Move SmartSwitch to AIR FRY/STOVETOP, set the cooking temperature to 370 degrees F and the cooking time to 10 minutes. 3. Toss the food halfway through. Serve hot.

Per Serving: Calories 88; Fat 7.08g; Sodium 143mg; Carbs 4.28g; Fiber 3.2g; Sugar 1.21g; Protein 3.97g

Nutmeg Apple Chips

Prep Time: 5 minutes | Cook Time: 9 minutes | Serves: 4

2 large sweet, crisp apples, cored and sliced
1 teaspoon ground cinnamon
½ teaspoon grated nutmeg
A pinch of salt

1.Toss the apple slices with the remaining ingredients. 2. Place the Crisper Tray in the bottom position. Arrange the apple slices on it in a single layer and close the lid. 3. Move SmartSwitch to AIR FRY/STOVETOP, set the cooking temperature to 390 degrees F and the cooking time to 9 minutes. Flip them halfway through. 4. Serve and enjoy.

Per Serving: Calories 61; Fat 0.3g; Sodium 40mg; Carbs 16.06g; Fiber 3.1g; Sugar 11.61g; Protein 0.33g

Crab Wontons

Prep Time: 15 minutes | Cook Time: 10 minutes | Serves: 5

4 ounces ⅓-less-fat cream cheese, at room temperature
2½ ounces (½ cup) lump crabmeat, picked over for bits of shell
2 scallions, chopped
2 garlic cloves, finely minced
2 teaspoons reduced-sodium soy sauce
15 wonton wrappers
1 large egg white, beaten
5 tablespoons Thai sweet chili sauce, for dipping

1. In a medium bowl, combine the cream cheese, crab, scallions, garlic, and soy sauce. Working with one at a time, place a wonton wrapper on a clean surface, the points facing top and bottom like a diamond. 2. Spoon 1 level tablespoon of the crab mixture onto the center of the wrapper. Dip your finger in a small bowl of water and run it along the edges of the wrapper. 3. Take one corner of the wrapper and fold it up to the opposite corner, forming a triangle. Gently press out any air between wrapper and filling and seal the edges. Set aside and repeat with the remaining wrappers and filling. 4. Brush both sides of the wontons with egg white. Arrange the wontons on the Crisper Tray in a single layer. Move SmartSwitch to AIR FRY/STOVETOP, set the cooking temperature to 340 degrees F and the cooking time to 8 minutes. 5. When done, the wontons should be golden brown and crispy. Serve the dish hot with the chili sauce for dipping.

Per Serving: Calories 241; Fat: 17.52g; Sodium: 539mg; Carbs: 9.84g; Fiber: 1.9g; Sugar: 3.56g; Protein: 10.72g

Seasoned Sweet Potato Chips

Prep Time: 10 minutes | Cook Time: 10 minutes | Serves: 3

2 large-sized sweet potatoes, peeled and cut into ¼-inch sticks
2 teaspoons olive oil
1 teaspoon garlic powder
1 tablespoon Mediterranean herb mix
Kosher salt and freshly ground black pepper, to taste

1. Toss the sweet potato with the remaining ingredients. 2. Place the Crisper Tray in the bottom position. Add the sweet potat sticks to it and close the lid. 3. Move SmartSwitch to AIR FRY/STOVETOP, set the cooking temperature to 360 degrees F an the cooking time to 15 minutes. 4. Toss the food halfway through. Serve and enjoy.

Per Serving: Calories 108; Fat 3.08g; Sodium 50mg; Carbs 19.06g; Fiber 2.9g; Sugar 3.76g; Protein 1.61g

Honey Pork Ribs

Prep Time: 5 minutes | Cook Time: 35 minutes | Serves: 4

2 pounds pork ribs
2 tablespoons honey
2 tablespoons butter
1 teaspoon sweet paprika
1 teaspoon hot paprika
1 teaspoon granulated garlic
Sea salt and ground black pepper, to taste
1 teaspoon brown mustard
1 teaspoon ground cumin

1. Toss all ingredients in a bowl. Place the Crisper Tray in the bottom position. 2. Add the pork ribs to it and close the li Move SmartSwitch to AIR FRY/STOVETOP, set the cooking temperature to 350 degrees F and the cooking time to 3 minutes. 3. Toss the food halfway through. Serve and enjoy.

Per Serving: Calories 409; Fat 18.88g; Sodium 214mg; Carbs 10.18g; Fiber 0.7g; Sugar 8.78g; Protein 47.58g

Savory Pumpkin Chips

Prep Time: 5 minutes | Cook Time: 13 minutes | Serves: 4

1 pound pumpkin, peeled and sliced
2 tablespoons coconut oil
1 teaspoon ground allspice
½ teaspoon chili powder
½ teaspoon garlic powder
½ teaspoon ground cumin
Sea salt and ground black pepper, to taste

1. Toss the pumpkin with the remaining ingredients until well coated on all sides. 2. Place the Crisper Tray in the botto position. Add the pumpkin slices to it and close the lid. 3. Move SmartSwitch to AIR FRY/STOVETOP, set the cookin temperature to 360 degrees F and the cooking time to 13 minutes. 4. Toss the food halfway through. Serve and enjoy.

Per Serving: Calories 716; Fat 62.6g; Sodium 302mg; Carbs 17.98g; Fiber 7.8g; Sugar 1.51g; Protein 34.09g

Crispy Green Beans

Prep Time: 5 minutes | Cook Time: 6 minutes | Serves: 4

½ cup flour
2 eggs, beaten
½ cup bread crumbs
½ cup Parmesan cheese, grated
½ teaspoon onion powder
¼ teaspoon cumin powder
½ teaspoon garlic powder
1 pound fresh green beans

1. In a shallow bowl, thoroughly combine the flour and eggs; mix to combine well. 2. In another bowl, mix the remaini ingredients. 3. Dip the green beans in the egg mixture, then, in the breadcrumb mixture. Place the Crisper Tray in t bottom position. 4. Add the green beans to it and close the lid. Move SmartSwitch to AIR FRY/STOVETOP, set the cookir temperature to 390 degrees F and the cooking time to 6 minutes. 5. Toss the food halfway through. Serve and enjoy.

Per Serving: Calories 180; Fat 6.43g; Sodium 281mg; Carbs 21.47g; Fiber 2.8g; Sugar 1.3g; Protein 9.71g

Fried Green Tomato Slices

Prep Time: 5 minutes | Cook Time: 15 minutes | Serves: 4

½ cup all-purpose flour
Sea salt and ground black pepper, to taste
1 teaspoon garlic powder
1 teaspoon cayenne pepper
2 eggs
½ cup milk
2 tablespoons olive oil
1 cup breadcrumbs
1 pound green tomatoes, sliced

1. In a shallow bowl, mix the flour, salt, black pepper, garlic powder, and cayenne pepper. 2. Whisk the egg and milk in another shallow bowl. Mix the olive oil and breadcrumbs in a separate bowl. 3. Dip the green tomatoes in the flour, then in the eggs, then in the breadcrumbs. Place the Crisper Tray in the bottom position. 4. Add the green tomato slices to it and close the lid. Move SmartSwitch to AIR FRY/STOVETOP, set the cooking temperature to 390 degrees F and the cooking time to 15 minutes. 5. Serve and enjoy.

Per Serving: Calories 249; Fat 13.41g; Sodium 135mg; Carbs 23.48g; Fiber 1.8g; Sugar 3.04g; Protein 9.35g

Beefsteak Tomato Chips

Prep Time: 10 minutes | Cook Time: 10 minutes | Serves: 2

1 beefsteak tomato, thinly sliced
2 tablespoons extra-virgin olive oil
Coarse sea salt and fresh ground pepper, to taste
1 teaspoon dried basil
1 teaspoon dried thyme
1 teaspoon dried rosemary

1. Toss the tomato slices with the remaining ingredients until they are well coated on all sides. 2. Place the Crisper Tray in the bottom position. Add the tomato slices to it and close the lid. 3. Move SmartSwitch to AIR FRY/STOVETOP, set the cooking temperature to 360 degrees F and the cooking time to 10 minutes. 4. When the cooking time is up, adjust the cooking temperature to 330 degrees F and cook them for 5 minutes more. 5. Serve and enjoy.

Per Serving: Calories 66; Fat 6.1g; Sodium 122mg; Carbs 2.76g; Fiber 0.7g; Sugar 1.35g; Protein 0.69g

Veggie Chicken Spring Rolls

Prep Time: 25 minutes | Cook Time: 15 minutes | Serves: 5

1 tablespoon toasted sesame oil
½ pound 93% lean ground chicken (see Skinny Scoop for vegetarian option)
4 tablespoons reduced-sodium soy sauce
1 teaspoon grated fresh ginger
3 garlic cloves, minced
2 large scallions, chopped
2 cups shredded napa or green cabbage
1 cup chopped baby bok choy
½ cup shredded carrots
1 tablespoon unseasoned rice vinegar
10 spring roll wrappers (8-inch square; made with wheat, not rice)
Olive oil spray
Thai sweet chili sauce, duck sauce, or hot sauce, for dipping (optional)

1. In a large skillet, heat the sesame oil over high heat. Add the chicken and 2 tablespoons of the soy sauce and cook them for 5 minutes until the chicken is just cooked through, breaking it up with a wooden spoon. 2. Add the ginger, garlic, and scallions, and cook them for 30 seconds until fragrant. Add the cabbage, bok choy, carrots, the remaining 2 tablespoons soy sauce, and the vinegar, and then cook them for 2 to 3 minutes until the vegetables are crisp-tender. Set aside to cool. 3. Working with one at a time, place a wrapper on a clean surface, the points facing top and bottom like a diamond. Spoon ¼ cup of the mixture onto the bottom third of the wrapper. 4. Dip your finger in a small bowl of water and run it along the edges of the wrapper. Lift the point nearest you and wrap it around the filling. 5. Fold the left and right corners in toward the center and continue to roll into a tight cylinder. Set aside and repeat with the remaining wrappers and filling. 6. Spray all sides of the rolls with oil. Transfer the rolls to the Crisper Tray. Move SmartSwitch to AIR FRY/STOVETOP, set the cooking temperature to 400 degrees F and the cooking time to 8 minutes. 7. Flip the food halfway through. You may need to cook the rolls in batches. Serve the dish with dipping sauce on the side, if desired.

Per Serving: Calories 241; Fat: 17.52g; Sodium: 539mg; Carbs: 9.84g; Fiber: 1.9g; Sugar: 3.56g; Protein: 10.72g

Tasty Potato Chips

Prep Time: 5 minutes | Cook Time: 16 minutes | Serves: 3

1 pound potatoes, thinly sliced
2 tablespoons olive oil
1 teaspoon paprika
Coarse salt and cayenne pepper, to taste

1. Toss the potatoes with the remaining ingredients. 2. Place the Crisper Tray in the bottom position. Add the potato slices t it and close the lid. 3. Move Smart Switch to AIR FRY/STOVETOP, set the cooking temperature to 350 degrees F and th cooking time to 16 minutes. 4. Toss the food halfway through. Serve and enjoy.

Per Serving: Calories 204; Fat 9.26g; Sodium 11mg; Carbs 28.25g; Fiber 3.8g; Sugar 2.02g; Protein 3.46g

Cauliflower Tots

Prep Time: 5 minutes | Cook Time: 10 minutes | Serves: 6-8

1 head of cauliflower
2 eggs
¼ cup all-purpose flour
½ cup grated Parmesan cheese
1 teaspoon salt
Freshly ground black pepper
Vegetable or olive oil, in a spray bottle

1. Grate the head of cauliflower with a box grater or finely chop it in a food processor. You should have about 3½ cups. Place the chopped cauliflower in the center of a clean kitchen towel and twist the towel tightly to squeeze all the water out the cauliflower. 3. Place the squeezed cauliflower in a large bowl. Add the eggs, flour, Parmesan cheese, salt and freshly grour black pepper. Shape the cauliflower into small cylinders or "tater tot" shapes, rolling roughly one tablespoon of the mixture a time. 4. Place the tots on a cookie sheet lined with paper towel to absorb any residual moisture. Spray the cauliflower tots a over with oil. Transfer the cauliflower tots to the Crisper Tray. 5. Move SmartSwitch to AIR FRY/STOVETOP, set the cookir temperature to 400 degrees F and the cooking time to 10 minutes. Flip the food halfway through. 6. Season with salt and blac pepper. Serve hot with your favorite dipping sauce.

Per Serving: Calories 241; Fat: 17.52g; Sodium: 539mg; Carbs: 9.84g; Fiber: 1.9g; Sugar: 3.56g; Protein: 10.72g

Cheeseburger Pockets

Prep Time: 5 minutes | Cook Time: 15 minutes | Serves: 4-6

1 pound extra lean ground beef
2 teaspoons steak seasoning
2 tablespoons Worcestershire sauce
8 ounces Cheddar cheese
⅓ cup ketchup
¼ cup light mayonnaise
1 tablespoon pickle relish
1 pound frozen bread dough, defrosted
1 egg, beaten
Sesame seeds
Vegetable or olive oil, in a spray bottle

1. Combine the ground beef, steak seasoning and Worcestershire sauce in a large bowl. Divide the meat mixture into 12 equ portions. 2. Cut the Cheddar cheese into twelve 2-inch squares, about ¼-inch thick. Stuff a square of cheese into the center each portion of meat and shape into a 3-inch patty. 3. Make the slider sauce by combining the ketchup, mayonnaise, and reli in a small bowl. Set aside. Cut the bread dough into twelve pieces. 4. Shape each piece of dough into a ball and use a rolli pin to roll them out into 4-inch circles. Dollop ½ teaspoon of the slider sauce into the center of each dough circle. 5. Place beef patty on top of the sauce and wrap the dough around the patty, pinching the dough together to seal the pocket shut. 6. T not to stretch the dough too much when bringing the edges together. Brush both sides of the slider pocket with the beaten eg 7. Sprinkle sesame seeds on top of each pocket. Transfer the slider pockets to the Crisper Tray. 8. Move SmartSwitch to AI FRY/STOVETOP, set the cooking temperature to 350 degrees F and the cooking time to 13 minutes. Flip the food after minutes of cooking time. You may need cook the pockets in batches. 9. When all the batches are done, pop all the sliders for few minutes to re-heat and serve them hot.

Per Serving: Calories 241; Fat: 17.52g; Sodium: 539mg; Carbs: 9.84g; Fiber: 1.9g; Sugar: 3.56g; Protein: 10.72g

Chili-Lime Polenta Fries

Prep Time: 10 minutes | Cook Time: 28 minutes | Serves: 4

2 teaspoons vegetable or olive oil
¼ teaspoon paprika
1 pound prepared polenta, cut into 3-inch x ½-inch sticks
salt and freshly ground black pepper
Chili-Lime Mayo:
½ cup mayonnaise
1 teaspoon chili powder
¼ teaspoon ground cumin
Juice of half a lime
1 teaspoon chopped fresh cilantro
Salt and freshly ground black pepper

1. Combine the oil and paprika and then carefully toss the polenta sticks in the mixture. Transfer the sticks to the Crisper Tray. 2. Move SmartSwitch to AIR FRY/STOVETOP, set the cooking temperature to 400 degrees F and the cooking time to 28 minutes. Flip the food after 15 minutes of cooking time. 3. Season to taste with salt and freshly ground black pepper. 4. To make the chili-lime mayo, combine all the ingredients in a small bowl and stir well. 5. Serve the polenta fries warm with chili-lime mayo on the side for dipping.
Per Serving: Calories 241; Fat: 17.52g; Sodium: 539mg; Carbs: 9.84g; Fiber: 1.9g; Sugar: 3.56g; Protein: 10.72g

Easy French Fries

Prep Time: 15 minutes | Cook Time: 25 minutes | Serves: 2-3

2 to 3 russet potatoes, peeled and cut into ½-inch sticks
2 to 3 teaspoons olive or vegetable oil
Salt

1. Bring a large pot of salted water to a boil while you peel and cut the potatoes. Blanch the potatoes in the boiling salted water for 4 minutes. Rinse them with cold water. 2. Dry them well with a clean kitchen towel. Toss the dried potato sticks gently with the oil and the transfer them to the Crisper Tray. 3. Move SmartSwitch to AIR FRY/STOVETOP, set the cooking temperature to 400 degrees F and the cooking time to 25 minutes. Toss the food a few times during cooking. 4. Season the fries with salt mid-way through cooking and serve them warm with tomato ketchup, Sriracha mayonnaise or a mix of lemon zest, Parmesan cheese and parsley. Yum!
Per Serving: Calories 241; Fat: 17.52g; Sodium: 539mg; Carbs: 9.84g; Fiber: 1.9g; Sugar: 3.56g; Protein: 10.72g

Chicken Wings with Blue Cheese Dip

Prep Time: 20 minutes | Cook Time: 25 minutes | Serves: 4

12 pieces (26 ounces) chicken wing portions
(a mix of drumettes and wingettes)
6 tablespoons Frank's RedHot sauce
2 tablespoons distilled white vinegar
1 teaspoon dried oregano
1 teaspoon garlic powder
½ teaspoon kosher salt
Blue Cheese Dip
¼ cup crumbled blue cheese
⅓ cup 2% Greek yogurt
½ tablespoon fresh lemon juice
½ tablespoon distilled white vinegar
2 celery stalks, halved crosswise and cut into 8 sticks total
2 medium carrots, peeled, halved crosswise and cut into 8 sticks total

1. In a large bowl, combine the chicken with 1 tablespoon of the hot sauce, the vinegar, oregano, garlic powder, and salt, tossing to coat well. 2. In a small bowl, mash the blue cheese and yogurt together with a fork. Stir in the lemon juice and vinegar until well blended. Refrigerate until ready to serve. 3. Transfer the chicken to the Crisper Tray. Move SmartSwitch to AIR FRY/STOVETOP, set the cooking temperature to 400 degrees F and the cooking time to 22 minutes. 4. Flip the food halfway through. Transfer the chicken to a large clean bowl. When all the batches are done, return all the chicken to the air fryer and cook for 1 minute to heat through. 5. Return the chicken to the bowl and toss with the remaining 5 tablespoons hot sauce to coat. 6. Arrange on a platter and serve with the celery, carrot sticks, and blue cheese dip.
Per Serving: Calories 241; Fat: 17.52g; Sodium: 539mg; Carbs: 9.84g; Fiber: 1.9g; Sugar: 3.56g; Protein: 10.72g

Clam Dip

Prep Time: 5 minutes | Cook Time: 12 minutes | Serves: 6

Cooking spray
2 (6.5-ounce) cans chopped clams, in clam juice
⅓ cup panko bread crumbs, regular or gluten-free
1 medium garlic clove, minced
1 tablespoon olive oil
1 tablespoon fresh lemon juice
¼ teaspoon Tabasco sauce
½ teaspoon onion powder
¼ teaspoon dried oregano
¼ teaspoon freshly ground black pepper
⅛ teaspoon kosher salt
½ teaspoon sweet paprika
2½ tablespoons freshly grated Parmesan cheese
2 celery stalks, cut into 2-inch pieces

1. Spray a suitable baking dish with cooking spray. Drain one of the cans of clams. 2. Place in a medium bowl along with the remaining can of clams (including the juice), the panko, garlic, olive oil, lemon juice, Tabasco sauce, onion powder, oregano, pepper, salt, ¼ teaspoon of the paprika, and 2 tablespoons of the Parmesan. 3. Mix well and let sit for 10 minutes. Transfer the food to the baking dish. Place the pan on the Crisper Tray, and then Roast them at 325 degrees F for 18 minutes. 4. Top them with the remaining ¼ teaspoon paprika and ½ tablespoon Parmesan after 10 minutes of cooking time. 5. Serve hot, with the celery for dipping.

Per Serving: Calories 241; Fat: 17.52g; Sodium: 539mg; Carbs: 9.84g; Fiber: 1.9g; Sugar: 3.56g; Protein: 10.72g

Garlicky Eggplant Chips

Prep Time: 5 minutes | Cook Time: 15 minutes | Serves: 4

1 pound eggplant, sliced
2 tablespoons olive oil
1 teaspoon garlic, minced
Sea salt and ground black pepper, to taste
2 tablespoons lemon juice, freshly squeezed

1. Toss the eggplant pieces with the remaining ingredients until they are well coated on all sides. 2. Place the Crisper Tray in the bottom position. 3. Add the eggplant pieces to it and close the lid. Move SmartSwitch to AIR FRY/STOVETOP, set the cooking temperature to 400 degrees F and the cooking time to 15 minutes. 4. Toss the food halfway through. Serve and enjoy.

Per Serving: Calories 91; Fat 6.98g; Sodium 3mg; Carbs 7.44g; Fiber 3.4g; Sugar 4.2g; Protein 1.19g

Fried Pickle Chips

Prep Time: 5 minutes | Cook Time: 12 minutes | Serves: 4

24 dill pickle slices
⅓ cup panko bread crumbs, regular or gluten-free
2 tablespoons cornmeal
1 teaspoon salt-free Cajun seasoning (I like the Spice Hunter)
1 tablespoon dried parsley
1 large egg, beaten
Olive oil spray
Cajun Buttermilk Ranch Dressing
⅓ cup 1% buttermilk
3 tablespoons light mayonnaise
3 tablespoons chopped scallion
¾ teaspoon salt-free Cajun seasoning
⅛ teaspoon garlic powder
⅛ teaspoon onion powder
⅛ teaspoon dried parsley
⅛ teaspoon kosher salt
Freshly ground black pepper

1. Place the pickles on paper towels to absorb the excess liquid, then pat them dry. In a medium bowl, combine the panko, cornmeal, Cajun seasoning, and parsley. 2. Put the egg in a separate small bowl. Working with one at a time, coat a pickle chip in the egg, then in the crumb mixture, gently pressing to adhere. 3. Set aside on a work surface and repeat with the remaining pickles. Spray both sides of the pickles with oil. 4. Transfer the chips to the Crisper Tray. Move SmartSwitch to AIR FRY/STOVETOP, set the cooking temperature to 400 degrees F and the cooking time to 8 minutes. Flip the food halfway through. 5. Meanwhile, whisk together the buttermilk, mayonnaise, scallion, Cajun seasoning, garlic powder, onion powder, dried parsley, salt, and pepper in a small bowl. 6. Serve alongside the pickles for dipping.

Per Serving: Calories 241; Fat: 17.52g; Sodium: 539mg; Carbs: 9.84g; Fiber: 1.9g; Sugar: 3.56g; Protein: 10.72g

Crab-Stuffed Mushrooms

Prep Time: 20 minutes | Cook Time: 10 minutes | Serves: 8

16 large white mushrooms
Olive oil spray
¼ teaspoon kosher salt
6 ounces (1 cup) lump crabmeat, picked over for bits of shell
⅓ cup freshly grated Parmesan cheese
¼ cup panko bread crumbs, regular or gluten-free
3 tablespoons mayonnaise
2 tablespoons chopped scallions
1 large egg, beaten
1 garlic clove, minced
¾ teaspoon Old Bay seasoning
1 tablespoon chopped fresh parsley
½ cup (2 ounces) shredded mozzarella cheese

1. Wipe the mushrooms with a damp paper towel to clean. Remove the stems, finely chop, and set aside. Spray the mushroom caps with oil and sprinkle with the salt. 2. In a medium bowl, combine the crab, Parmesan, panko, mayonnaise, chopped mushroom stems, scallions, egg, garlic, Old Bay, and parsley. Mound the filling (about 2 tablespoons each) onto each mushroom cap. 3. Top each with ½ tablespoon mozzarella, pressing to stick to the crab. Transfer the stuffed mushrooms to the Crisper Tray. 4. Move SmartSwitch to AIR FRY/STOVETOP, set the cooking temperature to 360 degrees F and the cooking time to 10 minutes. 5. When cooked, the mushrooms should be soft, the crab should be hot, and the cheese should be golden. Serve hot.

Per Serving: Calories 241; Fat: 17.52g; Sodium: 539mg; Carbs: 9.84g; Fiber: 1.9g; Sugar: 3.56g; Protein: 10.72g

Garlicky Knots

Prep Time: 25 minutes | Cook Time: 30 minutes | Serves: 8

1 cup (5 ounces) all-purpose or white whole wheat flour (see Skinny Scoop for gluten-free option), plus more for dusting
2 teaspoons baking powder
¾ teaspoon kosher salt
1 cup 0% Greek yogurt (not regular yogurt), drained of any liquid
Olive oil spray
2 teaspoons unsalted butter
3 garlic cloves, minced
1 tablespoon grated Parmesan cheese
1 tablespoon finely chopped fresh parsley
Warmed marinara sauce (optional), for serving

1. In a large bowl, whisk together the flour, baking powder, and salt. Add the yogurt and mix with a fork or spatula until well combined. 2. Lightly dust a work surface with flour. Transfer the dough to the work surface and knead for 2 to 3 minutes by hand until it is smooth and slightly tacky. 3. Divide the dough into 8 balls. Roll each ball into ropes, about 9 inches long. Tie each rope into a "knot" ball. Place on the work surface and spray the tops with olive oil. 4. Transfer the knots to the Crisper Tray. Bake them at 250 degrees F for 24 minutes. Remove from the basket and let cool for 5 minutes (they will continue cooking in the center). 5. Meanwhile, in a nonstick medium skillet, melt the butter over low heat. Add the garlic and cook, stirring frequently, until golden, about 2 minutes. 6. Toss the knots in the skillet with the melted butter and garlic. If the knots are too dry, give them another spritz of olive oil. 7. Sprinkle with the Parmesan and parsley. If desired, serve with marinara for dipping.

Per Serving: Calories 241; Fat: 17.52g; Sodium: 539mg; Carbs: 9.84g; Fiber: 1.9g; Sugar: 3.56g; Protein: 10.72g

Cheese Zucchini Chips

Prep Time: 5 minutes | Cook Time: 10 minutes | Serves: 4

1 pound zucchini, sliced
1 cup Pecorino Romano cheese, grated
Sea salt and cayenne pepper, to taste

1. Toss the zucchini slices with the remaining ingredients. 2. Place the Crisper Tray in the bottom position. Add the food to it in single layer and close the lid. Move SmartSwitch to AIR FRY/STOVETOP, set the cooking temperature to 390 degrees F and the cooking time to 10 minutes. 3. Toss the food halfway through. Serve and enjoy.

Per Serving: Calories 193; Fat 11.93g; Sodium 614mg; Carbs 6.13g; Fiber 1.4g; Sugar 0.88g; Protein 16.82g

Wonton Cups

Prep Time: 5 minutes | Cook Time: 10 minutes | Serves: 4

12 wonton wrappers
Olive oil spray
¾ cup dried beans (for weighting the cups)
2 tablespoons reduced-sodium soy sauce
1 teaspoon toasted sesame oil
½ teaspoon Sriracha sauce
¼ pound fresh sushi-grade ahi tuna, cut into ½-inch cubes
¼ cup peeled, seeded, and diced cucumber
2 ounces Hass avocado (about ½ small), cut into ½-inch cube
¼ cup sliced scallions
1½ teaspoons toasted sesame seeds

1. Place each wonton wrapper in a lined foil baking cup, pressing gently in the middle and against the sides to create a bowl. 2 Spray each lightly with oil. Add 1 heaping tablespoon of dried beans to the middle of each cup. Transfer the cups to the Crispe Tray. 3. Move SmartSwitch to AIR FRY/STOVETOP, set the cooking temperature to 280 degrees F and the cooking time t 10 minutes. Carefully remove the cups and let cool slightly. 4. Remove the beans and set the cups aside. In a medium bow combine the soy sauce, sesame oil, and Sriracha. Whisk well to combine. Add the tuna, cucumber, avocado, and scallions an toss gently to combine. 5. Add 2 heaping tablespoons of the ahi mixture to each cup and top each with ⅛ teaspoon sesam seeds. 6. Serve immediately.
Per Serving: Calories 241; Fat: 17.52g; Sodium: 539mg; Carbs: 9.84g; Fiber: 1.9g; Sugar: 3.56g; Protein: 10.72g

Tortillas Chips and Salsa

Prep Time: 15 minutes | Cook Time: 5 minutes | Serves: 4

Salsa:
¼ small onion
2 small garlic cloves
½ jalapeño, seeds and membranes removed (or leave in if you like it spicy)
1 (14.5-ounce) can diced tomatoes, undrained (not with basil; I like Tuttorosso)
Handful of fresh cilantro
Juice of 1 lime
¼ teaspoon kosher salt

Chips:
6 corn tortillas
Olive oil spray
¾ teaspoon chile-lime seasoning salt (such as Tajín or Trader Joe's)

1. In a food processor, combine the onion, garlic, jalapeño, tomatoes (including the juices), cilantro, lime juice, and salt. Puls a few times until combined and chunky (don't overprocess). 2. Transfer to a serving bowl. Spray both sides of the tortillas wit oil. Stack the tortillas on top of each other so they line up. 3. Using a large sharp knife, cut them in half, then in quarters, an once more so they are divided into 8 equal wedges each. 4. Spread out on a work surface and season both sides with chile lime salt. Transfer the tortilla wedges to the Crisper Tray. 5. Move SmartSwitch to AIR FRY/STOVETOP, set the cookin temperature to 400 degrees F and the cooking time to 5 minutes. Flip the food halfway through. 6. Let the dish cool a fe minutes before serving with the salsa.
Per Serving: Calories 241; Fat: 17.52g; Sodium: 539mg; Carbs: 9.84g; Fiber: 1.9g; Sugar: 3.56g; Protein: 10.72g

Hot Tortilla Chips

Prep Time: 5 minutes | Cook Time: 5 minutes | Serves: 4

9 corn tortillas cut into wedges
1 tablespoon olive oil
1 teaspoon hot paprika
Sea salt and ground black pepper, to taste

1. Toss the tortilla wedges with the remaining ingredients. 2. Place the Crisper Tray in the bottom position. Add the food to i and close the lid. Move SmartSwitch to AIR FRY/STOVETOP, set the cooking temperature to 360 degrees F and the cookin time to 5 minutes. 3. You can cook them in batches. Serve hot.
Per Serving: Calories 151; Fat 5.01g; Sodium 25mg; Carbs 24.78g; Fiber 3.7g; Sugar 0.54g; Protein 3.22g

Tomatillo Salsa Verde

Prep Time: 25 minutes | Cook Time: 10 minutes | Serves: 4

1 large poblano pepper
1 large jalapeño
¼ small onion
2 garlic cloves
Olive oil spray
¾ pound tomatillos (husks removed)
3 tablespoons chopped fresh cilantro
¼ teaspoon sugar (omit for keto diets)
1 teaspoon kosher salt

1. Spritz the poblano, jalapeño, onion, and garlic with olive oil, then transfer to the Crisper Tray. Cook for about 14 minutes, flipping halfway, until charred on top. (For a toaster oven–style air fryer, the temperature remains the same; cook for 10 minutes.) 2. Remove the poblano, wrap in foil, and let it cool for 10 minutes. Remove the remaining vegetables from the basket and transfer to a food processor. Spritz the tomatillos with oil. Transfer the food to the Crisper Tray. 3. Move SmartSwitch to AIR FRY/STOVETOP, set the cooking temperature to 400 degrees F and the cooking time to 10 minutes. Flip the food halfway through. 4. Transfer them to the food processor with the other vegetables. Unwrap the foil from the poblano. Peel the skin off and remove the seeds. 5. Transfer to the food processor along with the cilantro, sugar (if using), and salt. Pulse the mixture until the ingredients are coarsely chopped. 6. Add 5 to 6 tablespoons water and pulse until a coarse puree forms. Transfer the salsa to a serving dish.

Per Serving: Calories 241; Fat: 17.52g; Sodium: 539mg; Carbs: 9.84g; Fiber: 1.9g; Sugar: 3.56g; Protein: 10.72g

Homemade Devils on Horseback

Prep Time: 10 minutes | Cook Time: 7 minutes | Serves: 12

24 petite pitted prunes (4½ ounces)
¼ cup crumbled blue cheese (see Skinny Scoop for dairy-free option)
8 slices center-cut bacon, cut crosswise into thirds

1. Halve the prunes lengthwise, but don't cut them all the way through. Place ½ teaspoon of cheese in the center of each prune. Wrap a piece of bacon around each prune and secure the bacon with a toothpick. 2. Transfer the food to the Crisper Tray. Move SmartSwitch to AIR FRY/STOVETOP, set the cooking temperature to 400 degrees F and the cooking time to 7 minutes. 3. Flip the food halfway through. Let the dish cool slightly and serve warm.

Per Serving: Calories 241; Fat: 17.52g; Sodium: 539mg; Carbs: 9.84g; Fiber: 1.9g; Sugar: 3.56g; Protein: 10.72g

Loaded Zucchini Skins with Scallions

Prep Time: 25 minutes | Cook Time: 20 minutes | Serves: 4

3 slices center-cut bacon
2 large zucchinis (about 9 ounces each)
Olive oil spray
¾ teaspoon kosher salt
¼ teaspoon garlic powder
¼ teaspoon sweet paprika
Freshly ground black pepper
1¼ cups (5 ounces) shredded cheddar cheese
8 teaspoons light sour cream or 2% plain Greek yogurt
2 scallions, green tops only, sliced

1. Place the bacon in the Crisper Tray. Air-fry them at 350 degrees F for 10 minutes, flipping halfway, until crisp. Place the cooked bacon on paper towels to drain, then coarsely chop. 2. Halve the zucchini lengthwise, then crosswise (you'll have 8 pieces). Scoop the pulp out of each piece, leaving a ¼-inch shell on all sides (save the pulp for another use, such as adding to omelets or soup). 3. Place the zucchini skins on a work surface. Spray both sides with olive oil, then season all over with the salt. Season the cut side with the garlic powder, paprika, and pepper to taste. 4. Transfer the zucchini to the Crisper Tray. Move SmartSwitch to AIR FRY/STOVETOP, set the cooking temperature to 350 degrees F and the cooking time to 8 minutes. Flip the food halfway through. 5. Remove the zucchini from the basket and place 2½ tablespoons cheddar inside each skin and top with the bacon. Resume cooking them for 2 minutes until the cheese is melted. 6. Top each with 1 teaspoon sour cream and the scallions and serve immediately.

Per Serving: Calories 241; Fat: 17.52g; Sodium: 539mg; Carbs: 9.84g; Fiber: 1.9g; Sugar: 3.56g; Protein: 10.72g

Cheese Cauliflower Rice Arancini

Prep Time: 30 minutes | Cook Time: 30 minutes | Serves: 4

2 (2.75-ounce) sweet Italian chicken sausage links, casings removed
4½ cups riced cauliflower (frozen)
½ teaspoon kosher salt
1¼ cups marinara sauce
1 cup (4 ounces) shredded part-skim mozzarella cheese
Cooking spray
2 large eggs
½ cup bread crumbs, regular or gluten-free
2 tablespoons freshly grated Pecorino Romano or Parmesan cheese

1. Heat a large skillet over medium-high heat. Add the sausage and cook for 4 to 5 minutes until cooked through, breaking them up. Add the cauliflower, salt, and ¼ cup of the marinara. 2. Reduce the heat to medium and cook for 6 to 7 minutes until the cauliflower is tender and heated through, stirring occasionally. 3. Remove from the heat and add the mozzarella to the skillet, stirring well to mix. Let it cool slightly for 3 to 4 minutes until it's easy to handle with your hands but still hot. 4. Spray a ¼-cup measuring cup with cooking spray and pack tightly with the cauliflower mixture, leveling the top. 5. Use a small spoon to scoop it out into your palm and roll into a ball. Set aside on a dish. Repeat with the remaining cauliflower. 6. In a small bowl, beat the eggs with 1 tablespoon water until smooth. In a second bowl, combine the bread crumbs and pecorino. 7. Working one at a time, dip a cauliflower ball in the egg, then in the crumbs, gently pressing to adhere. Transfer to a work surface and spray all over with oil. 8. Repeat with the remaining cauliflower balls. Transfer the cauliflower balls to the Crisper Tray. 9. Move SmartSwitch to AIR FRY/STOVETOP, set the cooking temperature to 400 degrees F and the cooking time to 9 minutes. Flip the food halfway through. 10. When cooked, the crumbs should be golden and the center should be hot. Meanwhile, warm up the remaining 1 cup marinara for serving. 11. Serve the arancini with the warm marinara for dipping.
Per Serving: Calories 241; Fat: 17.52g; Sodium: 539mg; Carbs: 9.84g; Fiber: 1.9g; Sugar: 3.56g; Protein: 10.72g

Za'atar Chickpeas

Prep Time: 15 minutes | Cook Time: 12 minutes | Serves: 3

1 (15-ounce) can chickpeas, rinsed and drained*
⅛ teaspoon kosher salt
1 teaspoon za'atar spice blend
¼ teaspoon garlic powder
Extra-virgin olive oil spray

1. Place the chickpeas on a plate lined with paper towels. Pat with paper towels and let stand to dry completely. 2. In a small bowl, combine the salt, za'atar, and garlic powder. Transfer the chickpeas to the Crisper Tray. 3. Move SmartSwitch to AIR FRY/STOVETOP, set the cooking temperature to 375 degrees F and the cooking time to 12 minutes. Stir them every 5 minutes during cooking. 4. Transfer the chickpeas to a medium bowl. Lightly spray all over with olive oil and immediately toss with half of the spices while hot. 5. When the second batch is cooked, spray with oil and toss with the remaining spices. Let cool and eat at room temperature.
Per Serving: Calories 241; Fat: 17.52g; Sodium: 539mg; Carbs: 9.84g; Fiber: 1.9g; Sugar: 3.56g; Protein: 10.72g

Chapter 7 Dessert Recipes

Mini Apple Pies

Prep Time: 10 minutes | Cook Time: 10 minutes | Serves: 4

2 Granny Smith apples, peeled and diced
1 tablespoon unsalted butter, melted
2½ tablespoons evaporated cane sugar, divided
½ teaspoon ground cinnamon
⅛ teaspoon ground nutmeg
1 tablespoon freshly squeezed lemon juice
4 teaspoons water, divided
½ cup plain Greek yogurt
½ cup whole-wheat flour, plus more for dusting
1 egg

1. In a large bowl, mix together the apples, butter, 2 tablespoons of sugar, the cinnamon, nutmeg, lemon juice, and 3 teaspoons of water. Set aside. 2. In a medium bowl, mix together the yogurt, remaining ½ tablespoon of sugar, and the flour until a sticky dough forms. Divide the dough into 4 equal portions. Lightly dust a clean work surface with flour and roll out each dough portion into a 4-inch circle. 3. In a small bowl, whisk together the egg and the remaining 1 teaspoon of water to make an egg wash. 4. Divide the apple mixture between four 6-ounce ramekins. Top each ramekin with a dough circle. Brush the tops of the dough with the egg wash. Place the Crisper Tray in the bottom position. 5. Place the ramekins on the tray and close the lid. Move SmartSwitch to AIR FRY/STOVETOP, and then use the center front arrows to select BAKE/ROAST. 6. Set the cooking temperature to 350 degrees F and the cooking time to 10 minutes. Serve immediately.
Per Serving: Calories 165; Fat 3.66g; Sodium 36mg; Carbs 27.4g; Fiber 4.1g; Sugar 12.71g; Protein 6.77g

Mini Blackberry Pie

Prep Time: 10 minutes | Cook Time: 15 minutes | Serves: 6

1¼ cups whole-wheat flour, plus more for dusting
1 cup plain Greek yogurt
1 tablespoon honey
1 egg
1 teaspoon water
1 cup blackberries
⅛ cup evaporated cane sugar
1 tablespoon freshly squeezed lemon juice
1½ tablespoons cornstarch

1. In a medium bowl, combine the flour, yogurt, and honey until a dough forms. 2. Lightly dust a clean work surface with flour. Roll out the dough to a ¼-inch thickness and use a 4-inch round cookie cutter to cut out 6 rounds. You may need to reroll the dough scraps to get all 6 rounds. 3. In a small bowl, whisk together the egg and water to make an egg wash. Set aside. 4. In a medium bowl, mix together the blackberries, sugar, lemon juice, and cornstarch. Brush the outside edges of the dough rounds with the egg wash. 5. Place 2 heaping tablespoons of the blackberry mixture in the center of each circle. Fold over the dough into a half-moon and, using a fork, crimp the edges to seal. 6. Brush the tops of each pie with the egg wash. Place the Crisper Tray in the bottom position. Place the pies on the tray in single layer and close the lid. 7. Move SmartSwitch to AIR FRY/STOVETOP, and then use the center front arrows to select BAKE/ROAST. Set the cooking temperature to 375 degrees F and the cooking time to 12 minutes. 8. Turn the pies over after 7 minutes of cooking time. 9. Serve and enjoy. Leftovers can be stored in an airtight container at room temperature for up to 3 days.
Per Serving: Calories 182; Fat 2.72g; Sodium 34mg; Carbs 35.77g; Fiber 4.2g; Sugar 14.46g; Protein 6.22g

Banana Pastry Bites

Prep Time: 5 minutes | Cook Time: 20 minutes | Serves: 12

12 wonton wrappers
1 banana, cut into 12 pieces
½ cup peanut butter
Cooking oil

1. Lay out the wonton wrappers on a work surface. Place 1 banana slice and 1 teaspoon of peanut butter on each wrapper. 2. Fold each wrapper diagonally across to form a triangle. Bring the 2 bottom corners up toward each other. Do not close the wrapper yet. 3. Bring up the 2 open sides and push out any air. Squeeze the open edges together to seal. Place the Crisper Tray in the bottom position. 4. Add the food to it and close the lid. Move SmartSwitch to AIR FRY/STOVETOP, set the cooking temperature to 375 degrees F and the cooking time to 18 minutes. 5. Flip each bite over after 10 minutes of cooking time. 6. Cool the dish before serving.
Per Serving: Calories 133; Fat 2.43g; Sodium 344mg; Carbs 23.42g; Fiber 1g; Sugar 3.25g; Protein 4g

Carrot Cookie Bars

Prep Time: 25 minutes | Cook Time: 35 minutes | Serves: 8

8 tablespoons (1 stick) unsalted butter, melted
1 cup evaporated cane sugar
1 tablespoon blackstrap molasses
2 large eggs
2 teaspoons vanilla extract, divided
1 cup whole-wheat flour
½ teaspoon baking powder
1 teaspoon ground cinnamon
¼ teaspoon ground nutmeg
⅓ teaspoon salt
1 cup grated carrots
¼ cup chopped walnuts
4 ounces cream cheese, softened
2 tablespoons honey
Extra-virgin olive oil, in a spray bottle, for greasing

1. Whisk together the butter, sugar, and molasses in a large bowl. Add the eggs, one at a time, stirring between each addition. Add 1 teaspoon of vanilla and stir until combined. 2. In a medium bowl, sift together the flour, baking powder, cinnamon, nutmeg, and salt. Fold in the carrots and walnuts. 3. In a small bowl, mix together the cream cheese, honey, and remaining 1 teaspoon of vanilla until smooth. 4. Place the batter on the tray and top them with the cream cheese mixture, adding dollops randomly to cover the batter, and top with the remaining carrot bake batter; close the lid. 5. Move SmartSwitch to AIR FRY/STOVETOP, and then use the center front arrows to select BAKE/ROAST. Set the cooking temperature to 350 degrees F and the cooking time to 35 minutes. 6. When cooked, the toothpick inserted in the center of the cake should come out clean. Let the bars sit for 15 minutes. 7. Cut into 8 bars and serve. Leftovers can be stored in an airtight container in the refrigerator for up to 5 days.

Per Serving: Calories 275; Fat 14.97g; Sodium 177mg; Carbs 32.35g; Fiber 2.4g; Sugar 19.85g; Protein 4.67g

Dark Chocolate Cookies

Prep Time: 25 minutes | Cook Time: 5 minutes | Serves: 6

8 tablespoons (1 stick) unsalted butter
½ cup coconut sugar
1 tablespoon molasses
1 egg
1 teaspoon vanilla extract
1 cup whole-wheat flour
½ teaspoon baking soda
¼ teaspoon salt
½ cup dark chocolate chunks

1. Line the Crisper Tray with parchment paper. 2. In a large bowl, using an electric mixer to beat together the butter, coconut sugar, and molasses on medium speed until light and fluffy, about 3 minutes. 3. Add the egg and vanilla and beat until combined. Add the flour, baking soda, and salt and beat until combined. Fold in the chocolate chunks with a rubber spatula. 4. Divide the dough into 12 portions and place each portion on the parchment paper, leaving 1 inch between each cookie. 5. Move SmartSwitch to AIR FRY/STOVETOP, and then use the center front arrows to select BAKE/ROAST. Set the cooking temperature to 350 degrees F and the cooking time to 5 minutes. You can bake them in batches. 6. Transfer the cookies to a wire rack and let cool for at least 15 minutes before serving. 7. Leftovers can be stored in an airtight container in the refrigerator for up to a week.

Per Serving: Calories 289; Fat 16.06g; Sodium 269mg; Carbs 28.42g; Fiber 2.5g; Sugar 12.97g; Protein 8.7g

Cinnamon Donut Holes

Prep Time: 5 minutes | Cook Time: 10 minutes | Serves: 16

1 (8-ounce) can jumbo biscuit dough
Cooking oil
1 tablespoon stevia
2 tablespoons cinnamon

1. Form the biscuit dough evenly into 16 balls about 1 to 1½-inch thick. Place the Crisper Tray in the bottom position. 2. Add the donut holes to it and close the lid. Move SmartSwitch to AIR FRY/STOVETOP, set the cooking temperature to 360 degrees F and the cooking time to 8 minutes. 3. Flip the food halfway through. In a small bowl, combine the stevia and cinnamon and stir. 4. Spritz the donut holes with cooking oil. Dip the donut holes in the cinnamon and sugar mixture, and serve.

Per Serving: Calories 13; Fat 0.37g; Sodium 32mg; Carbs 4.12g; Fiber 0.6g; Sugar 0.28g; Protein 0.26g

Chocolate-Coconut Tart

Prep Time: 10 minutes | Cook Time: 20 minutes | Serves: 4

1 cup almond flour
¼ cup plus 2 teaspoons evaporated cane sugar, divided
4 tablespoons (½ stick) unsalted butter, melted
8 ounces dark chocolate
1 cup heavy (whipping) cream
2 egg yolks
¼ teaspoon salt
1 teaspoon vanilla extract
1 tablespoon maple syrup
¼ cup unsweetened coconut flakes

1. In a medium bowl, mix together the flour, 2 teaspoons of sugar, and the butter until crumbly. 2. Divide the mixture into 4 equal portions and press them into four 6-ounce ramekins. 3. Place the Crisper Tray in the bottom position. Place the ramekins on the tray and close the lid. Move SmartSwitch to AIR FRY/STOVETOP, and then use the center front arrows to select BAKE/ROAST. 4. Set the cooking temperature to 350 degrees F and the cooking time to 10 minutes. 5. Place the dark chocolate in a medium bowl. In a saucepan, heat the cream over medium heat, until simmering but not boiling. 6. Pour the cream over the dark chocolate, stirring constantly, until completely melted. Let cool for 3 minutes. 7. In a small bowl, whisk together the egg yolks, salt, remaining sugar, vanilla extract, and maple syrup, and then pour into the melted chocolate and mix until combined completely. 8. Pour the chocolate mixture equally into the ramekins and top each with a sprinkle of coconut flakes. 9. Bake them for 10 minutes more. Let the dish cool completely before refrigerating for at least 2 hours. 10. Serve chilled.

Per Serving: Calories 582; Fat 46.88g; Sodium 193mg; Carbs 33.63g; Fiber 6.7g; Sugar 19.76g; Protein 7.07g

Cream Mango Cake

Prep Time: 25 minutes | Cook Time: 30 minutes | Serves: 6

Extra-virgin olive oil, in a spray bottle, for greasing
4 tablespoons (½ stick) unsalted butter
¾ cup evaporated cane sugar
1 egg white
1½ cups whole-wheat flour
1 teaspoon baking soda
1 teaspoon salt
1 cup whole milk
2 teaspoons vanilla extract
1 cup diced mango

1. Spray a suitable baking pan with olive oil. Beat the butter, sugar, and egg white in a bowl. Add the flour, baking soda, salt, milk, and vanilla and beat until smooth. Fold in the mango. 2. Pour the batter into the prepared baking pan. Place the Crisper Tray in the bottom position. Place the pan on the tray and close the lid. 3. Move SmartSwitch to AIR FRY/STOVETOP, and then use the center front arrows to select BAKE/ROAST. Set the cooking temperature to 350 degrees F and the cooking time to 30 minutes. 4. When cooked, the toothpick inserted in the center should come out clean. Let cool on a wire rack for 15 minutes. 5. Remove the cake from the pan, cut into slices, and serve. Leftovers can be stored in an airtight container in the refrigerator for up to 3 days.

Per Serving: Calories 232; Fat 7.33g; Sodium 649mg; Carbs 37.42g; Fiber 3.7g; Sugar 15.55g; Protein 6.31g

Sweet Pistachio Cookies

Prep Time: 15 minutes | Cook Time: 20 minutes | Serves: 6

½ cup shelled raw pistachios, divided
½ cup almond flour
¼ cup evaporated cane sugar
1 egg white

1. In a food processor, pulse ¼ cup of pistachios until they are the size of crumbs. Be careful to not over-process into butter. 2. Chop the remaining pistachios into small pieces. In a large bowl, combine the processed pistachios, almond flour, sugar, egg white, and chopped pistachios and stir until well mixed. 3. Divide the dough into 6 portions. Place the Crisper Tray in the bottom position, and line it with parchment paper. Place the dough portions on the tray and close the lid. 4. Move SmartSwitch to AIR FRY/STOVETOP, and then use the center front arrows to select BAKE/ROAST. Set the cooking temperature to 375 degrees F and the cooking time to 7 minutes. 5. Let the cookies cool on a wire rack for 5 minutes before serving.

Per Serving: Calories 69; Fat 4.71g; Sodium 14mg; Carbs 4.96g; Fiber 1.1g; Sugar 2.91g; Protein 2.7g

Apple Hand Pies

Prep Time: 15 minutes | Cook Time: 20 minutes | Serves: 8

2 apples, cored and diced
¼ cup honey
1 teaspoon cinnamon
1 teaspoon vanilla extract
⅛ teaspoon nutmeg
2 teaspoons cornstarch
1 teaspoon water
4 frozen piecrusts, thawed if frozen hard
Cooking oil

1. Mix the cornstarch and water in a small bowl. Add the apples, honey, cinnamon, vanilla, and nutmeg to a saucepan over medium-high heat, and stir-fry them for 2 to 3 minutes until the apples are soft. 2. Add the cornstarch mix to the saucepan and cook them for 30 seconds. 3. Cut each piecrust into two 4-inch circles. Lay the piecrusts on a flat work surface. Mound ⅓ cup of apple filling on the center of each. 4. Fold each piecrust over so that the top layer of crust is about an inch short of the bottom layer. Tap along the edges of the top layer to seal. 5. Use the back of a fork to press lines into the edges. Place the Crisper Tray in the bottom position. 6. Place the pies on the tray and close the lid. Move SmartSwitch to AIR FRY/ STOVETOP. Set the cooking temperature to 400 degrees F and the cooking time to 10 minutes. 7. Cool the pies fully before serving.

Per Serving: Calories 97; Fat 2.43g; Sodium 47mg; Carbs 19.5g; Fiber 1.4g; Sugar 13.51g; Protein 0.48g

Cherry Turnovers

Prep Time: 15 minutes | Cook Time: 20 minutes | Serves: 8

1 (17-ounce) box frozen puff pastry dough, thawed
1 (10-ounce) can cherry pie filling
1 egg white, beaten
Cooking oil

1. Cute each dough into 4 squares for 8 squares total. 2. Spoon ½ to 1 tablespoon of cherry pie filling onto the center of each square. Do not overfill or the filling will leak out the turnover. 3. Brush the edges of the squares with the egg white. Fold the dough over diagonally to close each turnover. 4. Using the back of a fork, press lines into the open edges of each turnover to seal. 5. Place the Crisper Tray in the bottom position. Place the turnovers on the tray and close the lid. Move SmartSwitch to AIR FRY/STOVETOP, and then use the center front arrows to select BAKE/ROAST. 6. Set the cooking temperature to 370 degrees F and the cooking time to 8 minutes. 7. Let the food cool for 3 to 4 minutes before serving.

Per Serving: Calories 375; Fat 22.99g; Sodium 163mg; Carbs 37.13g; Fiber 1.1g; Sugar 0.48g; Protein 4.98g

Cheese Pineapple Wontons

Prep Time: 5 minutes | Cook Time: 40 minutes | Serves: 10

8 ounces cream cheese
1 cup finely chopped fresh pineapple (canned, drained pineapple can be used)
20 wonton wrappers
Cooking oil

1. In a small, microwave-safe bowl, heat the cream cheese in the microwave for 20 seconds to soften. 2. In a medium bowl, combine the cream cheese and pineapple. Stir to mix well. 3. Lay out the wonton wrappers on a work surface. A clean table or large cutting board works well. 4. Spoon 1½ teaspoons of the cream cheese and pineapple mixture onto each wrapper. Be careful not to overfill. 5. Fold each wrapper diagonally across to form a triangle. Bring the 2 bottom corners up toward each other. Do not close the wrapper yet. Bring up the 2 open sides and push out any air. 6. Squeeze the open edges together to seal. Place the Crisper Tray in the bottom position. Add the food to it and close the lid. 7. Move SmartSwitch to AIR FRY/ STOVETOP, set the cooking temperature to 380 degrees F and the cooking time to 18 minutes. 8. Flip the wontons after 10 minutes of cooking time. 9. Cool before serving.

Per Serving: Calories 268; Fat 7.47g; Sodium 465mg; Carbs 41.76g; Fiber 1.4g; Sugar 4.39g; Protein 7.99g

Crunch S'mores

Prep Time: 5 minutes | Cook Time: 3 minutes | Serves: 4

12 whole cinnamon graham crackers
2 (1.55-ounce) chocolate bars, broken into 12 pieces
12 marshmallows

1. Halve each graham cracker into 2 squares. 2. Place the Crisper Tray in the bottom position. Place the graham cracker squares on the tray and close the lid. 3. Move SmartSwitch to AIR FRY/STOVETOP, and then use the center front arrows to select BAKE/ROAST. Set the cooking temperature to 350 degrees F and the cooking time to 3 minutes. 4. Add a marshmallow onto each piece of melted chocolate after 2 minutes. 5. Top the dish with the remaining graham cracker squares and serve.
Per Serving: Calories 417; Fat 13.82g; Sodium 234mg; Carbs 71.5g; Fiber 3.4g; Sugar 37.23g; Protein 4.89g

Chocolate Jumbo Donuts

Prep Time: 5 minutes | Cook Time: 20 minutes | Serves: 8

1 (8-ounce) can jumbo biscuits
Cooking oil
Chocolate sauce, such as Hershey's

1. Separate the biscuit dough into 8 biscuits and place them on a flat work surface. 2. Cut a hole in the center of each biscuit. Place the Crisper Tray in the bottom position. 3. Add the daunts to it and close the lid. Move SmartSwitch to AIR FRY/STOVETOP, set the cooking temperature to 360 degrees F and the cooking time to 8 minutes. 4. Flip the donuts halfway through. Drizzle chocolate sauce over the donuts and enjoy while warm.
Per Serving: Calories 96; Fat 3.13g; Sodium 267mg; Carbs 15.27g; Fiber 0.4g; Sugar 0.99g; Protein 1.76g

Oat Blueberry Crisp

Prep Time: 5 minutes | Cook Time: 15 minutes | Serves: 8

1 cup rolled oats
½ cup all-purpose flour
¼ cup extra-virgin olive oil
¼ teaspoon salt
1 teaspoon cinnamon
⅓ cup honey
Cooking oil
4 cups blueberries (thawed if frozen)

1. Combine the rolled oats, flour, olive oil, salt, cinnamon, and honey in a large bowl. 2. Spray a suitable pan with cooking oil all over the bottom and sides of the pan. 3. Spread the blueberries on the bottom of the barrel pan and top them with the oat mixture. Place the Crisper Tray in the bottom position. 4. Place the pan on the tray and close the lid. Move SmartSwitch to AIR FRY/STOVETOP, and then use the center front arrows to select BAKE/ROAST. 5. Set the cooking temperature to 350 degrees F and the cooking time to 15 minutes.
Per Serving: Calories 169; Fat 4.05g; Sodium 133mg; Carbs 36.25g; Fiber 4g; Sugar 19.06g; Protein 3.47g

Cinnamon Apple Wedges

Prep Time: 10 minutes | Cook Time: 18 minutes | Serves: 4

4 large apples
2 tbsp. olive oil
½ cup dried apricots, chopped
1-2 tbsp. sugar
½ tsp. ground cinnamon

1. Peel the apples and slice them into eight wedges. Throw away the cores. Coat the apple wedges with the oil. Transfer the apple wedges to the Crisper Tray. 2. Move SmartSwitch to AIR FRY/STOVETOP, and then use the center front arrows to select BAKE/ROAST. Set the cooking temperature to 350 degrees F and the cooking time to 18 minutes. 3. Add the apricots after 15 minutes of cooking time. Stir together the sugar and cinnamon. Sprinkle this mixture over the cooked apples before serving.
Per Serving: Calories 241; Fat: 17.52g; Sodium: 539mg; Carbs: 9.84g; Fiber: 1.9g; Sugar: 3.56g; Protein: 10.72g

Bananas with Chocolate Sauce

Prep Time: 10 minutes | Cook Time: 10 minutes | Serves: 6

1 large egg
¼ cup cornstarch
¼ cup plain bread crumbs
3 bananas, halved crosswise
Cooking oil
Chocolate sauce

1. Beat the egg in a small bowl. In another bowl, place the cornstarch. Place the bread crumbs in a third bowl. 2. Dip the bananas in the cornstarch, then the egg, and then the bread crumbs. Place the Crisper Tray in the bottom position. 3. Add the food to it and close the lid. Move SmartSwitch to AIR FRY/STOVETOP, set the cooking temperature to 350 degrees F and the cooking time to 7 minutes. 4. Flip the food after 5 minutes of cooking time. Transfer the bananas to plates. 5. Drizzle the chocolate sauce over the bananas, and serve.

Per Serving: Calories 103; Fat 1.2g; Sodium 36mg; Carbs 22.37g; Fiber 1.8g; Sugar 8.03g; Protein 1.73g

Easy Chocolate Brownies

Prep Time: 10 minutes | Cook Time: 25 minutes | Serves: 6

Vegetable oil
½ cup (1 stick) unsalted butter
½ cup chocolate chips
3 large eggs
½ cup sugar
1 teaspoon pure vanilla extract

1. Generously grease a suitable baking pan with vegetable oil. 2. In a microwave-safe bowl, combine the butter and chocolate chips. 3. Microwave them on high for 1 minute. Stir them very well. In a medium bowl, combine the eggs, sugar, and vanilla. Whisk them until light and frothy. 4. While whisking continuously, slowly pour in the melted chocolate in a thin stream and whisk until everything is incorporated. 5. Pour the batter into the prepared pan. Place the Crisper Tray in the bottom position. 6. Place the pan on the tray and close the lid. Move SmartSwitch to AIR FRY/STOVETOP, and then use the center front arrows to select BAKE/ROAST. 7. Set the cooking temperature to 350 degrees F and the cooking time to 25 minutes. 8. When cooked, the toothpick inserted into the center should come out clean. 9. Let the dish cool in the pan on a wire rack for 30 minutes before cutting into squares.

Per Serving: Calories 167; Fat 12.09g; Sodium 21mg; Carbs 10.32g; Fiber 0.1g; Sugar 9.02g; Protein 2.09g

Coconut Banana Cake

Prep Time: 15 minutes | Cook Time: 60 minutes | Serves: 5

⅔ cup sugar, shaved
⅔ cup unsalted butter
3 eggs
1¼ cup flour
1 ripe banana, mashed
½ tsp. vanilla extract
⅛ tsp. baking soda
Sea salt to taste
Topping Ingredients:
Sugar to taste, shaved
Walnuts to taste, roughly chopped
Bananas to taste, sliced

1. Pre-heat the Air Fryer to 360°F. Mix together the flour, baking soda, and a pinch of sea salt. 2. In a separate bowl, combine the butter, vanilla extract and sugar using an electrical mixer or a blender, to achieve a fluffy consistency. Beat in the eggs one at a time. 3. Throw in half of the flour mixture and stir thoroughly. Add in the mashed banana and continue to mix. 4. Lastly, throw in the remaining half of the flour mixture and combine until a smooth batter is formed. Transfer the batter to a baking tray and top with the banana slices. 5. Scatter the chopped walnuts on top before dusting with the sugar. Place a sheet of foil over the tray and pierce several holes in it. 6. Transfer the food to the Crisper Tray. Move SmartSwitch to AIR FRY/STOVETOP, and then use the center front arrows to select BAKE/ROAST. 7. Set the cooking temperature to 360 degrees F and the cooking time to 48 minutes. When the cooking time is up, decrease the cooking temperature to 320 degrees F and cook for 10 minutes more until golden brown. 8. Insert a skewer or toothpick in the center of the cake. If it comes out clean, the cake is ready.

Per Serving: Calories 241; Fat: 17.52g; Sodium: 539mg; Carbs: 9.84g; Fiber: 1.9g; Sugar: 3.56g; Protein: 10.72g

Butter Almond Shortbread

Prep Time: 10 minutes | Cook Time: 12 minutes | Serves: 8

½ cup (1 stick) unsalted butter
½ cup sugar
1 teaspoon pure almond extract
1 cup all-purpose flour

1. In bowl of a stand mixer fitted with the paddle attachment, beat the butter and sugar on medium speed until light and fluffy, to 4 minutes. 2. Add the almond extract and beat for 30 seconds until combined. Turn the mixer to low. 3. Add the flour a litt at a time and beat for about 2 minutes more until well-incorporated. Place the Crisper Tray in the bottom position. 4. Place th dough on the tray and close the lid. Move SmartSwitch to AIR FRY/STOVETOP, and then use the center front arrows to sele BAKE/ROAST. 5. Set the cooking temperature to 375 degrees F and the cooking time to 12 minutes. 6. While the shortbrea is still warm and soft, cut it into 8 wedges. Let the dish cool in the pan on a wire rack for 5 minutes. 7. Remove the wedg from the pan and let cool completely on the rack before serving.

Per Serving: Calories 152; Fat 7.94g; Sodium 5mg; Carbs 18.19g; Fiber 0.4g; Sugar 6.16g; Protein 2.11g

Chickpea Brownies

Prep Time: 10 minutes | Cook Time: 20 minutes | Serves: 6

Vegetable oil
1 (15-ounce) can chickpeas, drained and rinsed
4 large eggs
⅓ cup coconut oil, melted
⅓ cup honey
½ cup chocolate chips
3 tablespoons unsweetened cocoa powder
1 tablespoon espresso powder (optional)
1 teaspoon baking powder
1 teaspoon baking soda

1. Generously grease a suitable baking pan with 4-inch sides with vegetable oil. 2. Combine the chickpeas, eggs, coconut oi honey, cocoa powder, espresso powder (optional), baking powder, and baking soda in a blender. Blend or process until smootl 3. Transfer the mixture to the prepared pan and stir in the chocolate chips. Place the Crisper Tray in the bottom position. Place the mold on the tray and close the lid. Move SmartSwitch to AIR FRY/STOVETOP, and then use the center front arrow to select BAKE/ROAST. Set the cooking temperature to 325 degrees F and the cooking time to 20 minutes. 5. When cooke the toothpick inserted into the center should come out clean. Let the dish cool in the pan on a wire rack for 30 minutes befor cutting into squares.

Per Serving: Calories 328; Fat 17.82g; Sodium 420mg; Carbs 36.3g; Fiber 5.6g; Sugar 19.13g; Protein 9.97g

Cute Strawberry Pies

Prep Time: 5 minutes | Cook Time: 10 minutes | Serves: 8

1 cup sugar
¼ tsp. ground cloves
⅛ tsp. cinnamon powder
1 tsp. vanilla extract
1 [12-oz.] can biscuit dough
12 oz. strawberry pie filling
¼ cup butter, melted

1. In a bowl, mix together the sugar, cloves, cinnamon, and vanilla. With a rolling pin, roll each piece of the biscuit dough int a flat, round circle. 2. Spoon an equal amount of the strawberry pie filling onto the center of each biscuit. Roll up the dough Dip the biscuits into the melted butter and coat them with the sugar mixture. 3. Coat with a light brushing of non-stick cookin spray on all sides. Transfer the cookies to the Crisper Tray. 4. Move SmartSwitch to AIR FRY/STOVETOP, and then use th center front arrows to select BAKE/ROAST. Set the cooking temperature to 340 degrees F and the cooking time to 10 minutes 5. Allow to cool for 5 minutes before serving.

Per Serving: Calories 241; Fat: 17.52g; Sodium: 539mg; Carbs: 9.84g; Fiber: 1.9g; Sugar: 3.56g; Protein: 10.72g

Coconut Chocolate Brownies

Prep Time: 10 minutes | Cook Time: 15 minutes | Serves: 8

½ cup coconut oil
2 oz. dark chocolate
1 cup sugar
2½ tbsp. water
4 whisked eggs
¼ tsp. ground cinnamon
½ tsp. ground anise star
¼ tsp. coconut extract
½ tsp. vanilla extract
1 tbsp. honey
½ cup flour
½ cup desiccated coconut
Sugar, to dust

1. Melt the coconut oil and dark chocolate in the microwave. Combine with the sugar, water, eggs, cinnamon, anise, coconut extract, vanilla, and honey in a large bowl. 2. Stir in the flour and desiccated coconut. Incorporate everything well. Lightly grease a baking dish with butter. 3. Transfer the mixture to the dish. Transfer the dish to the Crisper Tray. Move SmartSwitch to AIR FRY/STOVETOP, and then use the center front arrows to select BAKE/ROAST. 4. Set the cooking temperature to 350 degrees F and the cooking time to 15 minutes. Allow to cool slightly. Take care when taking it out of the baking dish. 5. Slice it into squares. Dust with sugar before serving.

Per Serving: Calories 241; Fat: 17.52g; Sodium: 539mg; Carbs: 9.84g; Fiber: 1.9g; Sugar: 3.56g; Protein: 10.72g

Banana Pastry Puffs

Prep Time: 10 minutes | Cook Time: 15 minutes | Serves: 8

1 package (8-oz.) crescent dinner rolls, refrigerated
1 cup milk
4 oz. instant vanilla pudding
4 oz. cream cheese, softened
2 bananas, peeled and sliced
1 egg, lightly beaten

1. Roll out the crescent dinner rolls and slice each one into 8 squares. Mix together the milk, pudding, and cream cheese using a whisk. 2. Scoop equal amounts of the mixture into the pastry squares. Add the banana slices on top. 3. Fold the squares around the filling, pressing down on the edges to seal them. Apply a light brushing of the egg to each pastry puff. Transfer the food to the Crisper Tray. 4. Move SmartSwitch to AIR FRY/STOVETOP, and then use the center front arrows to select BAKE/ROAST. Set the cooking temperature to 355 degrees F and the cooking time to 10 minutes.

Per Serving: Calories 241; Fat: 17.52g; Sodium: 539mg; Carbs: 9.84g; Fiber: 1.9g; Sugar: 3.56g; Protein: 10.72g

Chocolate Cake

Prep Time: 15 minutes | Cook Time: 45 minutes | Serves:8

½ cup sugar
1¼ cups flour
1 tsp. baking powder
⅓ cup cocoa powder
¼ tsp. ground cloves
⅛ tsp. freshly grated nutmeg
Pinch of table salt
1 egg
¼ cup soda of your choice
¼ cup milk
½ stick butter, melted
2 oz. bittersweet chocolate, melted
½ cup hot water

1. In a bowl, thoroughly combine the dry ingredients. In another bowl, mix together the egg, soda, milk, butter, and chocolate. 2. Combine the two mixtures. Add in the water and stir well. Take a suitable cake pan and transfer the mixture to the pan. Transfer the pan to the Crisper Tray. 3. Move SmartSwitch to AIR FRY/STOVETOP, and then use the center front arrows to select BAKE/ROAST. Set the cooking temperature to 320 degrees F and the cooking time to 45 minutes. 4. Frost the cake with buttercream if desired before serving.

Per Serving: Calories 241; Fat: 17.52g; Sodium: 539mg; Carbs: 9.84g; Fiber: 1.9g; Sugar: 3.56g; Protein: 10.72g

Oat Banana Cookies

Prep Time: 5 minutes | Cook Time: 15 minutes | Serves: 6

2 cups quick oats
¼ cup milk
4 ripe bananas, mashed
¼ cup coconut, shredded

1. Combine all of the ingredients in a bowl. Scoop equal amounts of the cookie dough onto a baking sheet. Transfer the shee to the Crisper Tray. 2. Move SmartSwitch to AIR FRY/STOVETOP, and then use the center front arrows to select BAKE ROAST. 3. Set the cooking temperature to 350 degrees F and the cooking time to 15 minutes.
Per Serving: Calories 241; Fat: 17.52g; Sodium: 539mg; Carbs: 9.84g; Fiber: 1.9g; Sugar: 3.56g; Protein: 10.72g

Pear & Apple Crisps

Prep Time: 5 minutes | Cook Time: 20 minutes | Serves: 6

½ lb. apples, cored and chopped
½ lb. pears, cored and chopped
1 cup flour
1 cup sugar
1 tbsp. butter
1 tsp. ground cinnamon
¼ tsp. ground cloves
1 tsp. vanilla extract
¼ cup chopped walnuts
Whipped cream, to serve

1. Lightly grease a baking dish and place the apples and pears inside. Combine the rest of the ingredients, minus the walnut and the whipped cream, until a coarse, crumbly texture is achieved. 2. Pour the mixture over the fruits and spread it evenly Top them with the chopped walnuts. Transfer the dish to the Crisper Tray. 3. Move SmartSwitch to AIR FRY/STOVETOP, an then use the center front arrows to select BAKE/ROAST. Set the cooking temperature to 340 degrees F and the cooking tim to 20 minutes. 4. Serve at room temperature with whipped cream.
Per Serving: Calories 241; Fat: 17.52g; Sodium: 539mg; Carbs: 9.84g; Fiber: 1.9g; Sugar: 3.56g; Protein: 10.72g

Berry Puffed Pastry

Prep Time: 5 minutes | Cook Time: 15 minutes | Serves: 3

3 pastry dough sheets
½ cup mixed berries, mashed
1 tbsp. honey
2 tbsp. cream cheese
3 tbsp. chopped walnuts
¼ tsp. vanilla extract

1. Roll out the pastry sheets and spread the cream cheese over each one. In a bowl, combine the berries, vanilla extract an honey. Cover a baking sheet with parchment paper. 2. Spoon equal amounts of the berry mixture into the center of each shee of pastry. Scatter the chopped walnuts on top. 3. Fold up the pastry around the filling and press down the edges with the bac of a fork to seal them. Transfer the sheet to the Crisper Tray. 4. Move SmartSwitch to AIR FRY/STOVETOP, and then use th center front arrows to select BAKE/ROAST. Set the cooking temperature to 375 degrees F and the cooking time to 15 minutes
Per Serving: Calories 241; Fat: 17.52g; Sodium: 539mg; Carbs: 9.84g; Fiber: 1.9g; Sugar: 3.56g; Protein: 10.72g

Milk Cherry Pie

Prep Time: 20 minutes | Cook Time: 15 minutes | Serves: 8

1 tbsp. milk
2 ready-made pie crusts
21 oz. cherry pie filling
1 egg yolk

1. Coat the inside of a pie pan with a little oil or butter and lay one of the pie crusts inside. Use a fork to pierce a few holes ir the pastry. 2. Spread the pie filling evenly over the crust. Slice the other crust into strips and place them on top of the pie filling to make the pie look more homemade. Transfer the food to the Crisper Tray. 3. Move SmartSwitch to AIR FRY/STOVETOP and then use the center front arrows to select BAKE/ROAST. Set the cooking temperature to 310 degrees F and the cooking time to 15 minutes. 4. Serve warm.
Per Serving: Calories 241; Fat: 17.52g; Sodium: 539mg; Carbs: 9.84g; Fiber: 1.9g; Sugar: 3.56g; Protein: 10.72g

Sweet Bananas

Prep Time: 5 minutes | Cook Time: 15 minutes | Serves: 4

4 ripe bananas, peeled and halved
1 tbsp. meal
1 tbsp. cashew, crushed
1 egg, beaten
1½ tbsp. coconut oil
¼ cup flour
1½ tbsp. sugar
½ cup friendly bread crumbs

1. Put the coconut oil in a saucepan and heat over a medium heat. Stir in the bread crumbs and cook for 4 minutes, stirring continuously. Transfer the bread crumbs to a bowl. 2. Add in the meal and crushed cashew. Mix them well. Coat each of the banana halves in the corn flour, before dipping it in the beaten egg and lastly coating it with the bread crumbs. 3. Transfer the coated banana halves to the Crisper Tray. Move SmartSwitch to AIR FRY/STOVETOP, and then use the center front arrows to select BAKE/ROAST. 4. Set the cooking temperature to 350 degrees F and the cooking time to 10 minutes.
Per Serving: Calories 241; Fat: 17.52g; Sodium: 539mg; Carbs: 9.84g; Fiber: 1.9g; Sugar: 3.56g; Protein: 10.72g

Butter Shortbread Fingers

Prep Time: 10 minutes | Cook Time: 12 minutes | Serves: 10

1½ cups butter
1 cup flour
¾ cup sugar
Cooking spray

1. In a bowl. combine the flour and sugar. Cut each stick of butter into small chunks. Add the chunks into the flour and the sugar. 2. Blend the butter into the mixture to combine everything well. Knead the mixture, forming a smooth consistency. 3. Shape the mixture into 10 equal-sized finger shapes, marking them with the tines of a fork for decoration if desired. Transfer the cookies to the Crisper Tray. 4. Move SmartSwitch to AIR FRY/STOVETOP, and then use the center front arrows to select BAKE/ROAST. Set the cooking temperature to 350 degrees F and the cooking time to 12 minutes. 5. Let cool slightly before serving. Alternatively, you can store the cookies in an airtight container for up to 3 days.
Per Serving: Calories 241; Fat: 17.52g; Sodium: 539mg; Carbs: 9.84g; Fiber: 1.9g; Sugar: 3.56g; Protein: 10.72g

Pumpkin Seeds & Cinnamon

Prep Time: 10 minutes | Cook Time: 15 minutes | Serves: 2

1 cup pumpkin raw seeds
1 tbsp. ground cinnamon
2 tbsp. sugar
1 cup water
1 tbsp. olive oil

1. In a frying pan, combine the pumpkin seeds, cinnamon and water. Boil the mixture over a high heat for 2 to 3 minutes. Pour out the water and place the seeds on a clean kitchen towel, allowing them to dry for 20-30 minutes. 2. In a bowl, mix together the sugar, dried seeds, a pinch of cinnamon and one tablespoon of olive oil. Transfer the food to the Crisper Tray. 3. Move SmartSwitch to AIR FRY/STOVETOP, and then use the center front arrows to select BAKE/ROAST. Set the cooking temperature to 340 degrees F and the cooking time to 15 minutes. 4. Stir the food a few times during cooking. Serve warm.
Per Serving: Calories 241; Fat: 17.52g; Sodium: 539mg; Carbs: 9.84g; Fiber: 1.9g; Sugar: 3.56g; Protein: 10.72g

Coconut Pineapple Sticks

Prep Time: 10 minutes | Cook Time: 10 minutes | Serves:4

½ fresh pineapple, cut into sticks
¼ cup desiccated coconut

1. Coat the pineapple sticks in the desiccated coconut. Transfer the food to the Crisper Tray. 2. Move SmartSwitch to AIR FRY/STOVETOP. Set the cooking temperature to 400 degrees F and the cooking time to 10 minutes. 3. Serve and enjoy.
Per Serving: Calories 241; Fat: 17.52g; Sodium: 539mg; Carbs: 9.84g; Fiber: 1.9g; Sugar: 3.56g; Protein: 10.72g

Lemon Tarts

Prep Time: 15 minutes | Cook Time: 15 minutes | Serves: 4

½ cup butter
½ lb. flour
2 tbsp. sugar
1 large lemon, juiced and zested
2 tbsp. lemon curd
Pinch of nutmeg

1. In a large bowl, combine the butter, flour and sugar until a crumbly consistency is achieved. Add in the lemon zest and juice, followed by a pinch of nutmeg. 2. Continue to combine. If necessary, add a couple tablespoons of water to soften the dough. Sprinkle the insides of a few small pastry tins with flour. 3. Pour equal portions of the dough into each one and add sugar or lemon zest on top. Transfer the lemon tarts to the Crisper Tray. 4. Move SmartSwitch to AIR FRY/STOVETOP, and then use the center front arrows to select BAKE/ROAST. Set the cooking temperature to 360 degrees F and the cooking time to 15 minutes. 5. Serve and enjoy.
Per Serving: Calories 241; Fat: 17.52g; Sodium: 539mg; Carbs: 9.84g; Fiber: 1.9g; Sugar: 3.56g; Protein: 10.72g

Vanilla Blueberry Pancakes

Prep Time: 10 minutes | Cook Time: 10 minutes | Serves: 4

½ tsp. vanilla extract
2 tbsp. honey
½ cup blueberries
½ cup sugar
2 cups + 2 tbsp. flour
3 eggs, beaten
1 cup milk
1 tsp. baking powder
Pinch of salt

1. Pre-heat the Air Fryer to 390°F. In a bowl, mix together all of the dry ingredients. Pour in the wet ingredients and combine with a whisk, ensuring the mixture becomes smooth. 2. Roll each blueberry in some flour to lightly coat it before folding it into the mixture. This is to ensure they do not change the color of the batter. 3. Coat the inside of a baking dish with a little oil or butter. Spoon several equal amounts of the batter onto the baking dish, spreading them into pancake-shapes and ensuring to space them out well. 4. Transfer the dish to the Crisper Tray. Move SmartSwitch to AIR FRY/STOVETOP, and then use the center front arrows to select BAKE/ROAST. Set the cooking temperature to 390 degrees F and the cooking time to 10 minutes. 5. Serve and enjoy.
Per Serving: Calories 241; Fat: 17.52g; Sodium: 539mg; Carbs: 9.84g; Fiber: 1.9g; Sugar: 3.56g; Protein: 10.72g

Butter Fritters

Prep Time: 20 minutes | Cook Time: 10 minutes | Serves:16

For the Dough:
4 cups flour
1 tsp. kosher salt
1 tsp. sugar
3 tbsp. butter, at room temperature
1 packet instant yeast
1¼ cups lukewarm water

For the Cakes
1 cup sugar
Pinch of cardamom
1 tsp. cinnamon powder
1 stick butter, melted

1. Place all of the ingredients in a large bowl and combine well. Add in the lukewarm water and mix until a soft, elastic dough forms. 2. Place the dough on a lightly floured surface and lay a greased sheet of aluminum foil on top of the dough. Refrigerate for 5 to 10 minutes. 3. Remove it from the refrigerator and divide it in two. Mold each half into a log and slice it into 20 pieces. 4. In a shallow bowl, combine the sugar, cardamom and cinnamon. Coat the slices with a light brushing of melted butter and the sugar. 5. Transfer the slices to the Crisper Tray. Move SmartSwitch to AIR FRY/STOVETOP, and then use the center front arrows to select BAKE/ROAST. 6. Set the cooking temperature to 360 degrees F and the cooking time to 10 minutes. Flip them halfway through cooking. 7. Dust each slice with the sugar before serving.
Per Serving: Calories 241; Fat: 17.52g; Sodium: 539mg; Carbs: 9.84g; Fiber: 1.9g; Sugar: 3.56g; Protein: 10.72g

Pumpkin Cake

Prep Time: 35 minutes | Cook Time: 15 minutes | Serves: 4

1 large egg
½ cup skimmed milk
7 oz. flour
2 tbsp. sugar
5 oz. pumpkin puree
Pinch of salt
Pinch of cinnamon (optional)
Cooking spray

1. Stir together the pumpkin puree and sugar in a bowl. Crack in the egg and combine using a whisk until smooth. Add in the flour and salt, stirring constantly. 2. Pour in the milk, ensuring to combine everything well. Spritz a baking tin with cooking spray. Transfer the batter to the baking tin. Transfer the tin to the Crisper Tray. 3. Move SmartSwitch to AIR FRY/STOVETOP, and then use the center front arrows to select BAKE/ROAST. 4. Set the cooking temperature to 350 degrees F and the cooking time to 15 minutes.

Per Serving: Calories 241; Fat: 17.52g; Sodium: 539mg; Carbs: 9.84g; Fiber: 1.9g; Sugar: 3.56g; Protein: 10.72g

Sponge Cake with Frosting

Prep Time: 35 minutes | Cook Time: 15 minutes | Serves: 8

For the Cake:
9 oz. sugar
9 oz. butter
3 eggs
9 oz. flour
1 tsp. vanilla extract
Zest of 1 lemon
1 tsp. baking powder

For the Frosting
Juice of 1 lemon
Zest of 1 lemon
1 tsp. yellow food coloring
7 oz. sugar
4 egg whites

1. Use an electric mixer to combine all of the cake ingredients. Grease the insides of two round cake pans. Pour an equal amount of the batter into each pan. Transfer the cake pans to the Crisper Tray. 2. Move SmartSwitch to AIR FRY/STOVETOP, and then use the center front arrows to select BAKE/ROAST. Set the cooking temperature to 320 degrees F and the cooking time to 15 minutes. You can cook them in batches. 3. In the meantime, mix together all of the frosting ingredients. Allow the cakes to cool. Spread the frosting on top of one cake and stack the other cake on top.

Per Serving: Calories 241; Fat: 17.52g; Sodium: 539mg; Carbs: 9.84g; Fiber: 1.9g; Sugar: 3.56g; Protein: 10.72g

Coco Lava Cake

Prep Time: 10 minutes | Cook Time: 12 minutes | Serves: 4

1 cup dark cocoa candy melts
1 stick butter
2 eggs
4 tbsp. sugar
1 tbsp. honey
4 tbsp. flour
Pinch of kosher salt
Pinch of ground cloves
¼ tsp. grated nutmeg
¼ tsp. cinnamon powder

1. Spritz the insides of four custard cups with cooking spray. Melt the cocoa candy melts and butter in the microwave for 30 seconds to 1 minute. 2. In a large bowl, combine the eggs, sugar and honey with a whisk until frothy. Pour in the melted chocolate mix. Throw in the rest of the ingredients and combine well with an electric mixer or a manual whisk. 3. Transfer equal portions of the mixture into the prepared custard cups. Transfer the cups to the Crisper Tray. 4. Move SmartSwitch to AIR FRY/STOVETOP, and then use the center front arrows to select BAKE/ROAST. Set the cooking temperature to 350 degrees F and the cooking time to 12 minutes. 5. Remove the cups from the Air Fryer and allow to cool for 5 to 6 minutes. Place each cup upside-down on a dessert plate and let the cake slide out. 6. Serve with fruits and chocolate syrup if desired.

Per Serving: Calories 241; Fat: 17.52g; Sodium: 539mg; Carbs: 9.84g; Fiber: 1.9g; Sugar: 3.56g; Protein: 10.72g

Cheese Strawberry Rolls

Prep Time: 10 minutes | Cook Time: 20 minutes | Serves: 12

1 (8-ounce) can crescent rolls
4 ounces cream cheese
1 tablespoon strawberry preserves
⅓ cup sliced fresh strawberries
Cooking oil

1. Roll out the dough into a large rectangle. Cut the dough into 12 rectangles by making 3 cuts crosswise and 2 cuts lengthwise. 2. Place the cream cheese in a small, microwave-safe bowl. Microwave the cream cheese for 15 seconds to soften. 3. In a medium bowl, combine the cream cheese and strawberry preserves and stir. 4. Scoop 2 teaspoons of the cream cheese and strawberry mixture onto each piece of dough. Spread, but avoid the edges of the dough. 5. Add 2 teaspoons of fresh strawberries to each. Roll up each of the rectangles to create a roll. Place the Crisper Tray in the bottom position. 6. Add the food to it and close the lid. Move SmartSwitch to AIR FRY/STOVETOP, set the cooking temperature to 350 degrees F and the cooking time to 8 minutes. 7. Cool before serving.

Per Serving: Calories 83; Fat 3.43g; Sodium 136mg; Carbs 10.42g; Fiber 0.5g; Sugar 2.02g; Protein 2.57g

Conclusion

Thank you for purchasing our cookbook! The Ninja Speedi Rapid Cooker and Air fryer is an advanced appliance. It has 12 cooking functions: Speedi meals, steam, and crisp, steam and bake, steam, proof, air fry, roast/bake, broil, dehydrate, sear/sauté, slow cook, and sous vide. The cleaning process is very simple. You can prepare any time of meals to use this appliance. In this cookbook, you will get delicious and every type of recipe you want. This appliance is perfect for those who have no time to cook for a long time. This appliance offers speedi meals to cook food quickly. If you don't have any knowledge of using this appliance, read this cookbook thoroughly. I hope you will get all answers that come to your mind. Thank you for appreciating us. Stay happy & good luck!

Appendix 1 Measurement Conversion Chart

WEIGHT EQUIVALENTS

US STANDARD	METRIC (APPROXINATE)
1 ounce	28 g
2 ounces	57 g
5 ounces	142 g
10 ounces	284 g
15 ounces	425 g
16 ounces (1 pound)	455 g
1.5pounds	680 g
2pounds	907 g

VOLUME EQUIVALENTS (DRY)

US STANDARD	METRIC (APPROXIMATE)
⅛ teaspoon	0.5 mL
¼ teaspoon	1 mL
½ teaspoon	2 mL
¾ teaspoon	4 mL
1 teaspoon	5 mL
1 tablespoon	15 mL
¼ cup	59 mL
½ cup	118 mL
¾ cup	177 mL
1 cup	235 mL
2 cups	475 mL
3 cups	700 mL
4 cups	1 L

TEMPERATURES EQUIVALENTS

FAHRENHEIT(F)	CELSIUS (C) (APPROXIMATE)
225 °F	107 °C
250 °F	120 °C
275 °F	135 °C
300 °F	150 °C
325 °F	160 °C
350 °F	180 °C
375 °F	190 °C
400 °F	205 °C
425 °F	220 °C
450 °F	235 °C
475 °F	245 °C
500 °F	260 °C

VOLUME EQUIVALENTS (LIQUID)

US STANDARD	US STANDARD (OUNCES)	METRIC (APPROXIMATE)
2 tablespoons	1 fl.oz	30 mL
¼ cup	2 fl.oz	60 mL
½ cup	4 fl.oz	120 mL
1 cup	8 fl.oz	240 mL
1½ cup	12 fl.oz	355 mL
2 cups or 1 pint	16 fl.oz	475 mL
4 cups or 1 quart	32 fl.oz	1 L
1 gallon	128 fl.oz	4 L

Appendix 2 Air Fryer Cooking Chart

Meat and Seafood	Temp	Time (min)
Bacon	400°F	5 to 10
Beef Eye Round Roast (4 lbs.)	390°F	45 to 55
Bone to in Pork Chops	400°F	4 to 5 per side
Brats	400°F	8 to 10
Burgers	350°F	8 to 10
Chicken Breast	375°F	22 to 23
Chicken Tender	400°F	14 to 16
Chicken Thigh	400°F	25
Chicken Wings (2 lbs.)	400°F	10 to 12
Cod	370°F	8 to 10
Fillet Mignon (8 oz.)	400°F	14 to 18
Fish Fillet (0.5 lb., 1-inch)	400°F	10
Flank Steak(1.5 lbs.)	400°F	10 to 14
Lobster Tails (4 oz.)	380°F	5 to 7
Meatballs	400°F	7 to 10
Meat Loaf	325°F	35 to 45
Pork Chops	375°F	12 to 15
Salmon	400°F	5 to 7
Salmon Fillet (6 oz.)	380°F	12
Sausage Patties	400°F	8 to 10
Shrimp	375°F	8
Steak	400°F	7 to 14
Tilapia	400°F	8 to 12
Turkey Breast (3 lbs.)	360°F	40 to 50
Whole Chicken (6.5 lbs.)	360°F	75

Desserts	Temp	Time (min)
Apple Pie	320°F	30
Brownies	350°F	17
Churros	360°F	13
Cookies	350°F	5
Cupcakes	330°F	11
Doughnuts	360°F	5
Roasted Bananas	375°F	8
Peaches	350°F	5

Frozen Foods	Temp	Time (min)
Breaded Shrimp	400°F	9
Chicken Burger	360°F	11
Chicken Nudgets	400°F	10
Corn Dogs	400°F	7
Curly Fries (1 to 2 lbs.)	400°F	11 to 14
Fish Sticks (10 oz.)	400°F	10
French Fries	380°F	15 to 20
Hash Brown	360°F	15 to 18
Meatballs	380°F	6 to 8
Mozzarella Sticks	400°F	8
Onion Rings (8 oz.)	400°F	8
Pizza	390°F	5 to 10
Pot Pie	360°F	25
Pot Sticks (10 oz.)	400°F	8
Sausage Rolls	400°F	15
Spring Rolls	400°F	15 to 20

Vegetables	Temp	Time (min)
Asparagus	375°F	4 to 6
Baked Potatoes	400°F	35 to 45
Broccoli	400°F	8 to 10
Brussels Sprouts	350°F	15 to 18
Butternut Squash (cubed)	375°F	20 to 25
Carrots	375°F	15 to 25
Cauliflower	400°F	10 to 12
Corn on the Cob	390°F	6
Eggplant	400°F	15
Green Beans	375°F	16 to 20
Kale	250°F	12
Mushrooms	400°F	5
Peppers	375°F	8 to 10
Sweet Potatoes (whole)	380°F	30 to 35
Tomatoes (halved, sliced)	350°F	10
Zucchini (½-inch sticks)	400°F	12

Appendix 3 Recipes Index

Made in the USA
Las Vegas, NV
07 December 2024